Technology Assessment

In the series
Labor and Social Change,
edited by Paula Rayman and Carmen Sirianni

Technology Assessment
A Feminist Perspective

Janine Marie Morgall

Temple University Press
Philadelphia

Temple University Press, Philadelphia 19122
Copyright © 1993 by Temple University. All rights reserved
Published 1993
Printed in the United States of America

The paper used in this publication meets the minimum requirements
of American National Standard for Information Sciences—Permanence
of Paper for Printed Library Materials,
ANSI Z39.48-1984 ⊗

Library of Congress Cataloging-in-Publication Data
Morgall, Janine Marie, 1947–
    Technology assessment: a feminist perspective / Janine Marie
Morgall.
        p.   cm. — (Labor and social change)
    Includes bibliographical references (p.   ) and index.
    ISBN 1-56639-090-7 (cl : alk. paper). — ISBN 1-56639-091-5 (pb :
alk. paper)
    1. Technology assessment.   2. Feminism.   3. Technology—Social
aspects.   I. Title.   II. Series.
T174.5.M665   1993
303.48'3'082—dc20   93-9447

To my mother and father

Contents

Acknowledgments

A complete list of my sources of inspiration is impossible. It would be presumptuous of me to think that I could trace the flow of information that has been transformed into knowledge, or even to remember when and how it happened. In writing a book like this, which draws upon literature in several fields, I have necessarily accumulated a large number of intellectual debts. Various people have referred me to new work, challenged my interpretations, and offered encouragement in many ways. The influence of my teachers and colleagues, the intellectual stimulation of women's studies, the fields of sociology and policy research have all contributed to this work.

Saying thank you, although inadequate, is the only way I can express my appreciation. First and foremost I am indebted to the Department of Sociology at the University of Lund, in Sweden, for providing education, advice, encouragement, and support. I thank Anna-Lisa Lindén, Hilary Rose, Aant Elzinga, Birgit Krantz, and Sara Goodman for their critical comments on this manuscript; Andrew Jamison and Tarja Cronberg for informed, inspiring, and constructive critique at crucial times. A special thanks to Boel Berner, whose detailed comments, challenging questions, and constructive criticisms far exceeded academic obligation.

I thank my colleagues at the Institute of Social Pharmacy, Royal Danish School of Pharmacy in Copenhagen, who were a source of intellectual stimulation. Hanne Herborg's insight and intellect kept me on track whenever I threatened to jump the rails and head off in the wrong direction. I am grateful to Karen Steenhard for her language support and Patricia Sterling for her editing skills.

Last but not least, my sincere appreciation to Ron Eyerman, without whose guidance this book would still be a two-page outline. Ron's unobtrusive influence made me believe that all the good ideas were my own.

Abbreviations

CBA	cost-benefit analysis
CCT	controlled clinical trial
CEA	cost-effectiveness analysis
DES	diethylstilbestrol
EDP	electronic data processing
EC	European Community
FAST	Forecasting and Assessment in the Field of Science and Technology
FINRRAGE	Feminist International Network of Resistance to Reproductive and Genetic Engineering
GNP	gross national product
ILO	International Labor Office (Geneva)
INSERM	Institut National de la Santé et de la Recherche Medicale (National Institute of Health and Medical Research, France)
IVF	in vitro fertilization
MTA	medical technology assessment
NOW	National Organization for Women (U.S.)
OECD	Organization for Economic Cooperation and Development (international)
OTA	Office of Technology Assessment (U.S.)
PMV	postmortem maternal ventilation
R&D	research and development
RSA	Royal Society of Arts (U.K.)
SPRI	Swedish Planning and Rationalization Institute of Health Studies
STG	Stuurgroep Toekomstscenario's Gezondheidzong (Commission on Future Health Care Technologies, Holland)
TA	technology assessment
TAB	Technology Assessment Board (U.S.)
WHO	World Health Organization

Technology Assessment

Introduction
On the Importance of Gender Analysis

"Dazzled by so many and such marvelous inventions," remarks Gabriel García Márquez in *One Hundred Years of Solitude* (1970), "the people of Macondo did not know where their amazement began."

Looking at technology today, I can easily identify with the people of Macondo: marvelous inventions can indeed appear dazzling. However, years of studying women and technology have taught me that no matter how bright and promising technology may look on the surface, there is always a dark side. Therefore, my studies have been concerned with how the effects of technological development can be understood and potentially directed through technology assessment (TA): that is, the process of identifying and evaluating the impact of technological change. I find the study of TA in general a worthy endeavor, because the quality of all life depends on the success or failure of directing development, now and in the future. More specifically, my studies focus on how TA relates to women's lives. I question whether TA can understand technology aimed at use for or by women without specifically analyzing gender aspects.

My interest in women and technology stems from

more than a decade of research into the effects of technological change on women in the context of their productive and reproductive lives. In the course of my work I found that dissimilar technological developments seem to have similar (and often negative) effects on women. I made this observation when I began researching women and health, after studying technology in the labor market for many years. Another observation was that women and women's needs were invisible, except within feminist studies. This was true in both the development and the assessment of technology.

How can women be made visible? Is there any way to predict the negative results of technology? And, is there any way to intervene? These are the questions that motivated and inspired me to study and analyze the phenomenon of TA. This book represents the integration of several of my research interests: women, technology, health, and TA.

I am not the first to address these questions, either separately or together. Other feminists have emphasized the inclusion of more women in the fields of science and technology as a first priority in an attempt to influence (and change) technological development. Although I agree that encouraging more women to enter those fields is a necessary step, I believe that the process is too slow, given the speed with which technological change is affecting women today, particularly in the field of reproductive technology. The rapidity of this development, its pervasiveness, and the irreversibility of some of its effects make time a scarcity. Therefore, I conclude that a more expedient course is, first, to make TA more visible by critiquing it, and then to make women visible within TA through the introduction of a gender analysis. The central focus of this study is technology assessment and, secondarily, medical technology assessment (MTA). The overall goal is to develop a theoretically grounded, critical approach to TA and MTA from a feminist perspective.

Background

Technology is the result of a long research and development process that includes numerous choices along the way, a process in which women are not represented proportionally. The phenomena of TA and MTA are relevant for sociological inquiry because they represent recent events in this long history of technological development in society, and because they have the potential to influence technology's role in future social development. It will be interesting to see what role, if any, TA will play in guiding technological progress in society.

The diffusion of technology into all spheres of life has been followed by ambiguous, unexpected, and sometimes disastrous consequences. I view TA as a response to technological development which, in some cases, has gone too far too fast. On the one hand, TA is an expression of the desire to understand and control technological development, to predict its consequences, and to avoid irreparable damage (economic, environmental, and human). On the other hand, TA traditionally provided industry with methods to examine safety and efficacy and, later, with tools for analyzing the economic feasibility of new products and for avoiding possible litigation. TA has generated national as well as international interest. Both economic and human resources have increasingly been made available for establishing and institutionalizing TA and, more recently, MTA.

TA normally positions itself at the societal level, attempting to analyze and understand the consequences of either a general technological development or a specific technology. Institutionalized national and international TA and MTA can be seen as intimately connected to policy development and the decision-making process. Non-institutionalized TA—performed by unions, social movements, special interest groups, and academic departments—can be but is not always characterized as critical (that is, it addresses issues of power, control, and dominance) because it emphasizes a dialogue with users.

Not everyone supports TA. Critics argue that it attempts to slow down progress and, at times, to inhibit innovation or even stop technological development. Advocates say it attempts to direct those processes, that assessment has been made necessary by public criticism and pressure from special interest groups in response to accidents, disasters, and the undesired social effects of technology.

The increasingly widespread interest in TA over the past thirty years can be explained by several factors: numerous international scandals concerning technology; industry's need to predict social development and areas of public concern; criticism of the direction of technological development by various special interest groups; a flagging economy in the industrialized world which has limited spending, making industry more aware of the need for successful product development and marketing. The most recent wave of public concern can be traced back to the 1960s and early 1970s, when interest in technology development often arose from spontaneous social protest directed at specific or widespread grievances.[1]

Because the weak economy in the industrialized nations has limited both private and public spending, particularly heavy investment in new technology, assessment has acquired a screening as well as a priority-setting function; that is, the issue becomes which technology is affordable, rather than which technology is desirable.

My research shows that the introduction of new technology does not affect all members of society in the same way. The interplay between technological change and social change is complex, especially as it affects social relations, and the consequences can vary greatly from one group to another. Women have been noticeably absent from the various stages of technological development: research and development, diffusion, marketing, and assessment. At every stage the social meaning of technology is being constructed and reconstructed, and for this reason the study of technology's social impact should be a major consideration in modern society.

TA has been given priority as a tool for policy-making in most Western countries. It has been developing as an instrument for exercising political as well as social control over both existing and future technology. This development is not always met with enthusiasm. Industry sees either institutionalized or non-institutionalized TA as a hindrance to production and competition and as an attempt to control markets. It is important to study the potential and the limitations of TA and MTA in order to understand the mechanisms behind these diverging interests.

The Major Problems

As a sociologist, I see a major problem with TA and MTA in their lack of an explicit theoretical anchor. As a field of research, TA has neither a theoretical nor a methodological agreed-upon basis, and I see evidence that institutionalized forms are developing around methods with only an implicit or no theoretical basis at all. I argue that the validity of the assessment becomes questionable when such methods develop and in some cases even flourish. Sociology teaches us that theory is important for what we see and how we relate to what we see. Methods that ignore the impact of technology on women do so because their implicit theories are not equipped to deal with gender. I argue that to be an effective tool for a democratic society, TA must address the consequences of technology in the context of everyday life, including the realities of dominance, control, and conflicting values, which are the essence of gender analysis.[2] I argue that values are strongly influenced by gender as well as by the specific group in which one happens to live and work.

I argue further that in order to develop a critical TA, we must develop underlying theories capable of dealing with these realities. Because the predictive value of TA and MTA lies in the validity of such theories, future assessment efforts should be directed toward the development of a theoretical base, rather than proceeding solely as the proliferation of methods.

My second major criticism is that, in general, most assessment is not critical; that is, it tends to support and encourage innovations rather than questioning and challenging them. In other words, assessment works as quality control rather than critical challenge. In practice, this approach encourages adaptation rather than a search for alternatives or an outright rejection of new technology. I argue that this is a result of the overall approach, which at times reduces political conflicts to technical problems. It is also a result of the choice of methods employed, which are seemingly atheoretical yet whose "knowledge interests" reflect the desire to influence and coerce behavior rather than contribute to the autonomy of the users (whether workers, patients, consumers, or women).[3] In addition, I argue that if TA ignores the gender typing in technological development, it can support and contribute to existing forms of women's oppression in the reproductive as well as the productive sphere.

The Major Questions

The primary question addressed by this study is, what constitutes critical TA and MTA?

Further questions are these: How are TA and MTA organized and practiced? Why is a gender analysis important? What can feminist studies contribute to the further development of TA and MTA? What should the elements of a critical TA and MTA be?

In answering these questions and attempting to contribute to the further development of TA and MTA, I try to provide an understanding of why and how TA and MTA evolved; identify the role of social movements and pressure groups in the development of TA and MTA; distinguish between various approaches and knowledge interests as they affect methods of TA and MTA; identify the strengths and limitations of TA and MTA's approach and methods; identify problems of public participation in the TA and MTA process; identify areas where technology has had a special impact on women; identify areas of feminist studies that can contribute to a critical TA and MTA; identify and criticize assessments that include gender; formulate guidelines and criteria for a critical TA and MTA; identify areas of research in need of development.

I criticize present forms of TA and MTA because most lack a gender analysis.[4] I propose to show that by ignoring gender, one ignores the power, control, and knowledge interests involved in technological development. The relevance of this study lies in its attempt to provide women (as well as other subordinate people) with tools for understanding and influencing TA and MTA.[5] I believe that what can be said here about women and technology may be applicable for other groups in society, although perhaps not in identical form.

Building on my own research and work experience, my approach is critical, sociological, and feminist. It examines the impact of social structure as well as women's perceptions of social reality. For a sociologist with a feminist perspective,[6] TA must address the question, how does or will this technology affect women? It must then ask, why is this so? and then, what serves women best? A feminist perspective necessitates putting the lifestyles, activities, and interests of more than half the population in the forefront of the analysis. A critical sociologist and feminist is interested in doing research that contributes to a body of knowledge whose aim is to elicit change in oppressive social and economic conditions.

By studying technology assessment from a critical

and feminist perspective, I propose to bring to light issues of dominance, control, and conflicting values that have relevance for TA in general.

My Study

I have initiated and been involved in various studies that examined the relationship between technological change and the potential for either liberation or control in two areas of women's lives: the productive and reproductive spheres. In the former, I have studied the introduction of computer technology within the clerical sector; in the latter, I have looked at reproductive technology within the health care sector. This book is a further development of my work, with special emphasis on the phenomena of TA and MTA.

Part I introduces systematically organized TA and MTA as they evolved from early warning systems to a broader-based analysis of social consequences. It goes on to describe the organization of TA and MTA; to outline frequently used methods of assessment and their limitations; and to discuss some practical problems perceived by TA's proponents, such as how to involve the public and who should represent the public. Where relevant, woman-related examples have been purposely selected as points of illustration.

In Part II, dealing with women and technology, I argue that both technological development and TA have grown, at least in part, from male interests and that this fact has implications that affect women's lives. I introduce the feminist research on technological development, followed by a feminist approach to TA and MTA. I identify a variety of feminist perspectives on technological development and discuss the tension between them. I distinguish my approach to TA from a purely feminist TA, which I find too narrow in scope. The purpose of Part II is to develop a theoretical basis that builds on critical as well as feminist scholarship.

Part III presents examples of technologies that have especially affected women. I draw on empirical data taken from my own research as well as other relevant studies to illustrate the gender-specific effects of (1) the introduction of technology—typewriters, computers, and scientific management—into the clerical sector; and (2) past and present trends in reproductive technology, such as contraception, treatment for infertility, prenatal screening, and birth technology. In the former, the consequences for women differ from those for men; in the latter, most of the technology is aimed exclusively at women. The purpose of Part III is to demonstrate through concrete examples the necessity of analyzing technology in the context of everyday life, and to demonstrate how a critical feminist approach can contribute to a more nuanced assessment.

The Conclusion attempts to consolidate some criteria for what I consider a critical TA and MTA.

This book, relying on nonfeminist as well as feminist analysis, has resulted in an approach to assessment that views technology as a dependent variable; regards technological change as a means to eliminate, weaken, or reinforce existing systems of control or, alternatively, to establish new ones; considers technological solutions as only *one* strategy among many for solving problems; stresses the importance of analyzing nontechnical factors in the development and introduction of a particular type of technology; emphasizes need analysis, historic analysis, and gender-specific analysis; sees systems of dominance (including patriarchal relations) as within rather than separate from capitalist development.

I wrote this book because I believe that having a voice in the assessment process *will* make a difference.

PART I
Technology
Assessment

1
Evolution

Technology assessment is a recent step in the overall process of technological development, a step that I view as a political response to public criticism of technology and its social applications. Technology is more than technique; in fact, in this study I often refer to it as social process. I begin this chapter with my definitions of technology and TA, then examine how TA evolved and the forms it has taken.

In the English language, "technology" was originally a term that signified the study of or discourse on art, both fine and applied. By the late nineteenth century it had come to mean the pursuit of results, especially the useful results of scientific research. By the twentieth century scientific research and technical invention had become interdependent: as science became more technological (through the development of increasingly sophisticated instruments and tools), technology became more scientific (STG 1987).

As a concept, technology came to refer not only to the logical products of science but also to the attitudes, processes, artifacts, and consequences associated with it. Thus the concept of technology prevalent today involves an extension of human facilities—that is, human strength and human capabilities—by means of *technique* (tools, machines, devices), *knowledge* (the specific knowledge and knowledge interests that become embodied in specific techniques), and *organization* (the ensuing systematic procedure or mode of work that accompanies the use of the techniques).

Technology in this sense developed as a product of scientific rationalism and industrial capitalism in Europe and North America, often in close relation with military research and development. Technology today is substantially different from that produced by pre- or nonindustrial societies, not only in its origins and its application, but in its claim that it can solve many human problems as well as technical ones. It encompasses the social relations involved in creating, changing, and sharing (or monopolizing) knowledge about techniques. Technology is introduced and disseminated, and its use regulated, through rational organization and the capitalist mode of production. In addition to a close and productive relationship between science and military power,[1] one can see several simultaneous developments that contributed to the present concept of technology as technique, knowledge, and organization: (1) a scientific revolution, the influence of rational philosophy, and the general acceptance of the mechanistic paradigm;[2] (2) an economic revolution and changes in social relations which created a favorable economic and organizational climate: that is, private financing of scientific research for industrial purposes; and (3) an industrial revolution, whereby the application of technology became utilitarian, pragmatic, rational, and of service to profit-making.

It is important to mention here (although it is discussed in more detail in Part II) that Western science and technology have a long-standing tradition as masculine endeavors.

Definition

Technology assessment is usually positioned at the societal level. In the commonly agreed upon definition, TA is the attempt to analyze and understand the consequences of a specific technology or a technological trend. Traditionally, it served an early warning function, providing society with information from which precautions could be taken. Subsequently, this simple definition has been elaborated to include the various interpretations of what a relevant assessment encompasses.

The American Office of Technology Assessment (OTA) defines technology assessment as "a comprehensive form of policy research that examines the technical, economic, and social consequences of technological applications. It is especially concerned with unintended, indirect, or delayed social impacts" (quoted in STG 1987). As such, TA aims to identify all the possible impacts of a new technology, not just those intended. It includes the effects that cannot be measured quantitatively, as well as those that can (Hetman 1973). It can also be regarded as a process of cultural evaluation by which a nation or any cultural unit reflects upon the implications of particular technological choices (Jamison and Baark 1990). It can be seen as a process of political choices being made about technology, forcing people to rethink their value preferences (Brooks 1973). It can also be seen as a means of neutralizing reactions and responses to social debates about technology.[3]

Although there has never been an agreed-upon theoretical basis or method of analysis for TA, visible avenues of development can be found. Two clearly distinct trends are *policy orientation* and *research orientation*.[4]

In its policy-oriented form, TA is described in the narrow sense as the evaluation or testing of technology for safety, cost, and efficacy (benefits). In its broader sense, it is a comprehensive form of policy research that examines the technical, economic, and social consequences of technical application and attempts to anticipate the need for regulation. This form of TA has been guided by narrowly circumscribed methodologies for forecasting the environmental, economic, and social impact of technological change. Usually carried out by industry or within national and international institutions, it has sought to promote itself as an objective, politically neutral tool. The popular perception of TA derives almost exclusively from this form.

Research-oriented TA as it currently exists is what Jamison and Baark (1990) characterize as an open-ended discussion of technological options which focuses on societal and political implications. This form is often carried out by social actors, including social movements and pressure groups seeking to influence and control the course of technological development. It is most often within this form that the body of feminist work on TA is found.

History

An essential feature of the Industrial Revolution was the rapid and dramatic advance of technology. Following major breakthroughs in power (energy-generating) methods, production, and the military sector, there was an almost unanimous general enchantment with the wonders of technology. But not all members of society met these developments with the same enthusiasm; though the nineteenth century spawned technological optimism, the voices of dissent grew louder and louder. Organized resistance began with industrial workers' demands for the suppression of machinery. For them, technology was a symbol of yet another power factor in their lives and a loss of control over their labor.

Among the best-known cases of resistance were the "machine bashing" of the Luddite rebellion and the sabotage of Belgian weavers. The Luddite uprising took place among English textile workers during the years 1811 to 1816; it was a violent outbreak against laborsaving machinery by disgruntled workers who felt that their jobs, wages, and way of life were being threatened by the Industrial Revolution (Rybczynski 1983).[5] Nineteenth-century Belgian weavers "accidentally" dropped their heavy wooden clogs, called sabots, into the looms, giving birth to the term "sabotage."

Demonstrative resistance and dissent have continued to the present day in the form of individual as well as organized protest.[6] More prevalent, however, has been the attempt to exert influence over the control of technology through government regulation and institutionalized TA: "Regulation of technology has evolved in response to growing public awareness of the consequences of technical change and a desire for greater public accountability by government and industry" (Coombs, Saviotti, and Walsh 1987, 254). Since the mid-1960s, rapidly growing public, political, and scholarly interest has resulted in "a rapid proliferation of new legislation to regulate technology and to create new bureaucracies to refine and enforce the regulations" (Brooks 1976, 17).

This interest can be explained by the flagging economy in the industrialized world. Limited resources require difficult decisions with regard to government spending and make industry more and more aware of the need for efficient product development and marketing. Pressure from special interest groups, international scandals involving technology, ignorance, and inadequate or meaningless assessments have also made industry the target of litigation. The sluggish attitude of both private and public sectors about informing the public of side effects of certain technologies and the resultant damage, exposed in the international media, subsequently formed the basis of social protest. Widely publicized scandals of a general nature include the pollution of the environment as a result of industrial waste released into the ocean and the soil, acid rain, nuclear accidents,[7] the occupational health hazards of asbestos[8] and epoxy,[9] and the release of nerve-destroying gases into the atmosphere. Of a more specific nature (and of special interest to women) were the scandals within the medical industry concerning the side effects of birth control pills[10] and thalidomide.[11]

Between the 1950s and the 1970s in the industrialized world, the unquestioning acceptance of technological change as beneficial and progressive gradually became tempered by concern. In the 1960s and early 1970s, technology was blamed for many problems, for unexpected consequences, and for an increased lack of control. Pollution, loss of privacy with the proliferation of data banks, so-called technological unemployment resulting from automation, the depletion and possible exhaustion of natural resources, and the threat of nuclear war were focuses of this concern. It found expression in the platforms and programs of political parties, trade unions, social movements, and pressure groups.

An example from environmentalism occurred in 1962 when *Silent Spring* by Rachel Carson was published and changed the way many people thought about the world in which they lived. The book was unusual in that it was a critique of the chemical pesticide industry written for the public in "nonscientific" language. The author's argument was that synthetic poisons ignored the realities of biology and created even worse insect problems than before. The impact was tremendous; despite the controversy generated (that is, the backlash from the chemical industry), it is one of the most influential books on the environment to date. It became a catalyst for the American environmental movement and provoked the creation of the federal Environmental Protection Agency (EPA), as well as inspiring laws to prevent deterioration of the environment (Cramer, Eyerman, and Jamison 1987).

The desire for social control of the direction of technological development emerged from the general public's increasing awareness of the consequences of poor planning. There was a gap, however, between this awareness and the actual establishment of a public-minded TA, which did not come about until the 1970s. At that point science and technology policy began to move into new phases that affected industry. For example, new research councils were set up in Scandinavia, and the space program began mobilizing industrial research in the United States.

Systematic TA is relatively recent. I have divided its development in the industrialized Western countries into two chronological phases, pre- and post-1970s. Phase one, when TA was a goal-oriented tool for companies and narrowly defined interest groups, gradually gave way to phase two, in which the emphasis was on a broader-based assessment of consequences, more and more often funded by public means. What follows is a general overview of TA in the West, which has been both policy- and research-oriented. It would be necessary to analyze the culture-specific combination of the two orientations for any study of TA at the national level.

Early and Later Forms

Technology assessment was originally defined by industry as an analytic discipline used to determine and support decisions about which products and processes should be prioritized and developed. In manufacturing, the same results can often be achieved through different means: for example, tools can be produced mechanically, hydraulically, or electromagnetically. The same product can frequently be manufactured by completely different technologies: for example, as a result of genetic engineering, some vaccines can today be produced both chemically and biotechnically. In cases like these, a choice must often be made to pursue one or the other technological development. This need to choose between methods places TA at the very heart of the production process.

In its early form, economic formulations and priorities were frequently used methods in TA: cost-benefit analysis, program planning and budgeting systems, program evaluation and review techniques. Most significantly, these methods were characteristic of certain (often national) industries such as the American aerospace industry and the French electronics industry.

Assessing technology has always been a major concern for industry, although not always practiced in a systematically organized form or defined in the same words. From the beginning, industry had its own TA capability, carrying out tests for safety and efficacy in the form of quality control as well as examining the economic feasibility of new products.

Industrial TA has traditionally been the domain of engineers, technicians, and, later, economists. Long-term planning is necessary if profits are to be made. Investments in new technology in industry must be carefully calculated if financial disaster is to be avoided. Financial disaster encompasses not only loss from a product that fails to sell but also the costs involved in litigation when an accident or damage results from a product, or the fines imposed by the government for negligence in the workplace or general environment. TA has often been seen as a preventive measure. For this reason, privately based research and development (R&D) as well as government organizations have contributed much to this field. Military R&D in particular has throughout history pervaded and played a major role in directing technology and more recently TA.[12] In fact, since World War II as much as 40 percent of R&D worldwide has been devoted to the military (Wajcman 1991).

Voluntary organizations too have been responsible for various assessments of specific aspects of technology. One such example is the Birth Control Investigation Committee in the United Kingdom, which researched hormones as early as the 1930s—more than twenty years before the investigations carried out by the pharmaceutical industry (Walsh 1980).

During phase one, in short, TA was focused on industrial policy issues. It was ad hoc, narrowly confined to safety, efficacy, and cost-benefit analysis; was isolated either within industries or among special interest and pressure groups; had no formal systematic control from outside; was carried out primarily by engineers, technicians, and functionaries; involved little or no international cooperation; and evoked limited public concern and influence.

With time, institutions and groups outside the market began to work for the control of technology. In fact, the commercialization of technology, especially biotechnology, is regarded as a major factor in the later development of TA (Dickson 1984). Initially, assessing biotechnology was almost exclusively a matter for scientists themselves. Then, as the technology progressed through the innovative process, economic actors and business firms became increasingly involved. With the commercialization of genetic engineering in the 1970s, however, the *nature* of the issues shifted from internal to external (Jamison and Baark 1990), and TA increasingly became a matter of public policy and interest.

Until this time, the citizens in countries with market economies and democratically elected governments had usually accepted that government policy with regard to technical change was the province of elected representatives. But as various segments of public opinion—in unions, pressure groups, social movements, and so on—became convinced that the combination of market forces and governmental policy had been inadequate,

> widespread public concern about such unwanted effects of technical change as environmental pollution, unsafe products or work hazards obliged governments to tighten up their legislation on these issues. Neither market forces nor existing laws were regarded as adequate to protect the pub-

lic from the unwanted consequences of technical change. The agent of change was that rather hard-to-define entity "public opinion" reflected in, and reinforced by, the mass media and the campaigns of pressure groups and political parties. [Coombs, Saviotti, and Walsh 1987, 255–56]

The result of this increased attention was the growth of TA in both institutionalized and non-institutionalized contexts.

Institutionalized TA

Phase two witnessed an expansion of science and technology policy characterized by expensive new agencies. In Sweden, for example, councils were established to give each sector its own science and technology policy.

By the late 1960s, influential scientific bodies were recognizing the growing concern over "society's seeming inability to channel technological developments in directions that sufficiently respect the broad range of human needs" (U.S. Congress 1969; quoted in OECD 1983). Among research policy-makers, this gave rise to a number of conceptual and analytical activities concerning impact assessment and its usefulness in predicting consequences and formulating policies.

In the 1960's and early 1970's, technology assessment was mainly viewed, by policy-makers and analysts alike, as a brake on the introduction of technologies likely to prove harmful in environmental or social terms. But more recently [late 1970s], there has been an inclination to search for better economic results by foreseeing obstacles to technological innovation beforehand. In addition, the available experience of assessment studies suggests a gradual shift from cost-benefit analysis to a form of policy analysis. The new approach is to view assessment of technological impacts as a specific process rather than as an analytical tool and to search for positive outcomes as well as controlling for negative impacts. Technology assessment in this new form is much less controversial than before because attitudes have converged on the need for a "foresight function" of some sort. [OECD 1983, p. 13]

In the 1970s a law was passed requiring companies with government contracts for American space and military programs to carry out TA. In fact, more than any other single factor, it was the U.S. space program that was responsible for the initial establishment of systematic TA. The aerospace industry was motivated more by economic and practical interests than by ideological concerns. In the late 1960s there had been a sudden interest among engineers to do "social projects," mainly because of cutbacks in the U.S. aerospace and defense firms in the mid-1960s. Approximately 120,000 jobs were lost in two years, and 4,000 jobs were being lost every month nationally. This "sudden interest" in social projects can be seen as a search for new markets (Elliott and Elliott, 1976). The subsequent influence of military thinking on the development and especially the methods of TA was substantial.

In 1972 the American Office of Technology Assessment (OTA) was established, and the Organization for Economic Cooperation and Development (OECD) set up a special program for the social assessment of technology. I have chosen these two organizations to illustrate institutionalized TA for the following reasons: they took the lead; they represent national and international efforts and have often served as models for both; and they illustrate some of the major issues and interests that are characteristic of phase two.[13]

Office of Technology Assessment
Rapid developments in the U.S. military and space programs during the 1960s and 1970s resulted in a sixfold increase in government spending for scientific research and development. At the same time, the U.S. Congress was being asked to allocate even more money to technological development without being able to foresee the outcome

clearly (Gibbons and Gwin 1988). It became necessary to formalize a competent, impartial body to advise Congress on the important physical consequences of the increasingly complex use of technology. In 1966 the House of Representatives Subcommittee on Science, Research, and Development published a report (U.S. Congress 1966) on the adverse effects of technological development. This report included a request for the establishment of an early warning system capable of uncovering the potential negative as well as positive effects of technology application.

The OTA was established by the Technology Assessment Act of 1972 as a special congressional agency to supply impartial information on the probable beneficial and adverse impacts of applications of technology, and to develop and coordinate information that could be of help to the Congress in its work. By the mid 1970s it had been allocated a budget of $8 million and had a professional staff of 100 people.

From the beginning, Congress emphasized that the assessments should not be narrowly confined to economic or purely national security issues but should also include the effects of technology on living conditions and regional differences. The motivations for this untraditional parliamentary initiative were many. First, some congressmen felt ill prepared to evaluate the management of funds by the government: "OTA was set up after Congress voted against the supersonic transport Lockheed L2000, intended to rival Concorde. Congress wanted independent advice and thought that the expert witnesses representing the Nixon administration and the aerospace industry made out a very biased case" (Coombs, Saviotti, and Walsh 1987, 240). Congress needed advice especially for items on the military budget, to help them determine which weapons projects were worth the money.[14]

Another motivation was that many in Congress did not feel that they could rely on "expert" testimony provided

by scientists, among others. When experts frequently dis-
agreed to the point that the "facts" were blatantly contradictory, "Congress soon realized that scientists too can be
politicized and that the needed 'facts' cannot be lifted directly from the scientific journals and plugged into the
policy debate" (Gibbons and Gwin 1988, 100).

A third factor in the debate was the more common-
place need to raise public consciousness and counter the
skeptical attitude toward applied science, as well as to
attend to a new urgency regarding problems of public
health and welfare.[15] The first director of the OTA, Emilio
Daddario, made Congress aware of this public distrust
(OTA 1972). He thought that TA directed by Congress, as
the forum of leadership closest to the people, could per-
suade the public that society directs technology, not the
other way around.

Over the years, the OTA promised to assess the consequences of potential new technology: for example, microelectronics. Congress has also used the agency's competence to illuminate the interaction between technology
development level, economic disposition, living conditions, and regional variations. In 1979 the OTA drew up a
list of thirty priority areas.[16] The OTA assessed existing
technology as well, focusing on traditional sectors such as
steel, coal production, and public administration, which
had been adversely affected by the economic downturn of
the times.

Of particular interest to women, the OTA has taken up
such areas as mammography and screening for breast
cancer, technology and childbirth, infertility and treatment. Related issues such as the use of fetal tissue, the
failure rates and lack of regulation of in vitro fertilization
clinics, medical insurance, and new reproductive technologies were the subjects of state and federal legislative
hearings in the late 1980s. Increasingly, women in general
and, in many cases, well-known feminists are being asked

to testify as experts for federal and state legislative hearings on these issues (Hynes 1989a).

The OTA serves as an example of organizing TA on a national level using an "independent TA body approach," in contrast to the "task force approach" adopted in the United Kingdom. (The Parliamentary Office of Science and Technology [POST] is the nearest British equivalent to the OTA; however, it does not have the financial support of the government. Dependent on outside funding and with a tiny staff, it cannot carry out TA independently but must rely on organizing task forces composed of specially convened panels or advisory boards.) It cannot be denied that a major objective of the OTA has been to strengthen the position of Congress in the decision-making process against that of the executive branch (Smits and Leyten 1988).

Organization for Economic Cooperation and Development
The OECD was established in 1960 as an international organization of industrialized countries for the purpose of promoting economic growth, contributing to economic expansion, and encouraging the expansion of world trade.[17]

In 1971 the OECD published the "Brooks Report" (OECD 1971), which encouraged member states to initiate studies on the unforeseen consequences of technology. It emphasized the potential role of practicing scientists in creating a better understanding of the control and acceptance of technology.

The OECD soon recognized the "need for new relationships between research, technological innovation and decision-making." After dealing with issues of scientific and technological innovation for many years, the organization found it necessary to "take into account not only technical and economic aspects but also the societal dimension of impacts of new technological development"; it defined the essential need as "some kind of social management of technology" (OECD 1983). And the fact that most modern technology was being developed by international organizations, chiefly business corporations, created a need to regulate agencies at the international level.

Several activities were initiated. As early as 1967 the OECD published a book on TA (Jantsch 1967) which proposed ways to transfer military future studies techniques to civil projects.[18] In 1973 an in-depth exploration of state-of-the-art TA was published (OECD 1973), and an attempt was made to set up guidelines for member countries (OECD 1975). The Advisory Group on Control and Management of Technology was established to inform the OECD Secretariat of the needs and wishes of member governments. An analysis of a number of existing studies considered to be representative of the TA activities in interested member countries was performed and later published (OECD 1978).

Enthusiasm was not a characteristic of OECD efforts at the start. Tuininga (1988) recalls his experience at early OECD expert meetings on TA as "gatherings of a diverse group of semi-interested officials or scientists." By the late 1970s, however, a change in approach could be observed:

> As more and more experience [was] gathered, it became clear that technology assessment was often hampered by the narrow perspective adopted by the first practitioners. With the emergence of the oil crisis and subsequent economic difficulties, governments in member countries turned their hopes to technological innovation as a major determinant of their economic dynamics and improved competitiveness. Consequently, a much broader and deeper assessment of new technological developments was advocated to encompass their discernible and relevant implications for society and to make possible their incorporation into the decision-making process at any significant level of society. [OECD 1983, 9]

The OECD has stayed with broad issues, perhaps because of its international perspective. These include defense, economic development of traditional industries such as agriculture and mining, and services such as communication and transportation (Tisdell 1981). The OECD has not taken up issues of particular interest to or relevance for women and has not put as much effort into health-related issues as the OTA. Still, overall agreement on and support of multidisciplinary TA can be seen today, not only in the OECD but in the OTA and other national programs as well.

Non-Institutionalized TA

The shift to a more social assessment which occurred in the mid-1970s has been interpreted as a response to mass "insecurity" among the public. This insecurity and the response of officials have been attributed not to planning and technological development as such but rather to a growing awareness that development should be planned for the people. Consequently, another characteristic of phase two was the growing influence of social movements and pressure groups whose collective action was aimed at social reorganization.[19] Although not a precise term, "social movements" as used in this study refers to large groups of people (usually not highly institutionalized) that become involved in seeking to accomplish or block a process of social change: for example, the women's movement, the peace movement, the environmental movement. What I call "pressure groups" tend to be more formally constituted organizations (sometimes within the larger movements) that are designed at least in part to bring pressure to bear on the government, the civil service, or other political institutions in order to achieve the ends they favor; national patients' associations and, in the United States, the National Organization for Women (NOW) are examples. As an illustration of the distinction,

I apply the term "social movement" to the women's movement in general and the term "pressure group" to an organization such as NOW within the women's movement. It should be noted that during this same period, academia was debating the origin and growth of science. The social constructionist analysis, which finds dominant social relations to be constitutive of science, undoubtedly influenced the direction TA took at this point.[20] The exploration of the relationship between science and ideology, also prevalent at this time (Rose and Rose 1976), likewise stimulated the activist demands being developed by social movements.[21]

Increasingly in the years since 1970, consumer groups have assessed products (usually for household use) with regard to the consequences for the user: that is, their quality and endurance, and their effects on consumer economy and living standards. Most Western countries are familiar with such consumer reports, which are regularly published in both specialized and general-interest magazines. This kind of assessment by and for interest groups, called "partisan" TA, is discussed later in more detail.

The demand for institutionalized TA was not an explicit priority of the social movements of the 1970s but rather a logical response to the issues they addressed, such as the development of safe energy sources, cuts in military expenditure, and safer reproductive technology. The women's movement of the 1960s and early 1970s criticized the ways in which technological development was affecting basic issues of reproduction: abortion, birth control, and the medicalization of the birth process. The movement saw many developments as threats to women's autonomy and as issues of power and control. Some feminists chose to work with labor unions and grassroots groups.[22] Like many other social movements, however, the women's movement never explicitly formulated demands for TA.

Although the attempt to influence government policy by pressure groups is a characteristic of phase two because it then became so widespread, it is not a new phenomenon. Already in the 1920s and 1930s, during phase one, campaigns for the legislation of birth control and the opportunity to make various methods more widely available were organized in the United States, the United Kingdom, France, and the Scandinavian countries. Over time, pressure groups interested in contraceptive technology became so successful that today they are no longer considered to be outside the system. That is, what began in the 1920s as a small number of family planning associations evolved into established, respected institutions operating nationally and internationally. Most recent and most radical is the Feminist International Network of Resistance to Reproductive and Genetic Engineering (FINRRAGE), which is highly critical of new reproductive technology (see Chapter 2).

In an essay on the consumer in the service society, Gartner (1982) discusses what he calls the upsurge of consumer power in the United States.[23] Quoting a 1977 nationwide survey of consumers and the consumer movement (Harris 1978), he finds the work of the movement to be a sign of consumers' unwillingness to leave the job of looking after their interests to those who have political and economic control. In its power and desire for change, he sees analogies between the consumer movement and the populists of the 1880s, the organization of industrial workers in the 1930s, and the civil rights movement of the 1960s.

Although consumer groups have achieved a certain degree of success by exerting pressure on legislators, their main influence has been achieved by providing information to consumers which enables them to make informed product choices. In some countries—Denmark, for example—this service is performed by a government department. In the United States, consumer pressure has been much more political.[24]

Other examples of the increase in public interest during phase two can be found within labor unions. Historically, the primary aim of trade unions has been to secure members' jobs and improve their wages. Initially, unions were not directly concerned with issues of technology; in fact, many trade unionists took the view that technological issues were outside their scope or even in conflict with their main aims. This changed when technological developments began to have a direct effect not only on union members' jobs, skills, and wages but on their health, safety, and the nature of their work (Coombs, Saviotti, and Walsh 1987). The shift in focus from salary negotiations to the betterment of work conditions can be seen in the unions' criticism of the effects of new technology in the 1970s, especially with regard to occupational health hazards (Morgall 1981c). Recent economic recession has made trade unions particularly conscious of the vulnerability even of large companies, the scale of unemployment, and the difficulty of finding new jobs in the wake of cutbacks and layoffs. In many countries, this awareness has resulted in the use of collective bargaining to influence the distribution of the benefits of technical change.[25]

It is characteristic of phase two that TA became a public concern. A closer interaction developed between policy-making initiatives and broader public debates about the particular technologies being assessed. National and international bodies began to develop TA as a tool to spread information and contribute to the understanding of technology and ways of organizing it. Attempts were made to move from "narrow" economic assessments toward multidisciplinary social assessments. Finally, attempts were made to involve the public in decision-making regarding the future of technology and society.[26] On the national and international levels, both the

OTA and the OECD have contributed to these efforts. Their numerous published studies and reports are notable for being informative and readable.

Summary

Technology involves more than physical objects or technique. It embodies social relations made up of knowledge interests and organizational planning and practice. This chapter links the origin and development of TA closely to social concerns, public resistance, and an increase in public demands for a say in technological development.

The history of systematic TA can be divided into two phases. In phase one (pre-1970s), TA was ad hoc, narrowly defined, often orthogonal to industrial technology policy, and without systematic control. It was practiced by a limited number of professional groups and was of little national and international interest.

In phase two (1970s onward), TA became a matter of public concern and more broadly based. TA is not a neutral tool. It has evolved in various forms which, on a national level, have been strongly influenced by cultural norms and values. Like technology itself, assessment is mediated by a complex process whose outcome depends on the relative strengths of the interested parties. Unless challenged and forced to act as an instrument for change, institutionalized TA will continue to develop as a support for current political policy. Social movements and pressure groups present a challenge to traditional and institutional TA. The involvement of the social and human sciences as well as the general public forces TA to address more than just technical issues.

National and international efforts have been made to meet the challenge of regulating and controlling technological development. Non-institutionalized TA has increased, including initiatives taken by social movements and pressure groups. A critical approach to science and technological development as well as institutionalized TA has also become a feature of these efforts.

In conclusion, it can be said that the need for TA has grown throughout the century, as technological progress became less and less transparent and more complex for both policy-makers and the public.

2
Organization

Although no country in the world today claims to have systematic, continuous evaluation of existing and emerging technology, it is everywhere a major concern. In some countries, TA has become institutionalized within special agencies or offices; in others, it is less explicit and carried out within a variety of organizational contexts (Jamison and Baark 1990). An important issue in the discussion about institutionalization concerns the power of TA agencies in decision-making. It appears that the form of the organization, its choice of tasks, and the influence and structure of scientific work are contributing factors (Tuininga 1988).

This chapter examines the following aspects of the organization of TA today: how and why governments organize and administer TA; how and why medical technology is being singled out and its assessment administered separately; the ways in which various sectors of the public are organizing and influencing TA; issues being addressed by women.

Institutionalized TA

Aside from the social conditions and pressures that led to an interest in controlling technology, other factors—some of them technical—have contributed to government involvement in doing so, which expanded considerably after World War II. In an attempt to explain government involvement in TA, Coombs, Saviotti, and Walsh (1987) outline what they call the five preconditions for government control of technology.

1 The recognition of an actual rather than a potential hazard. Historically, legislation has taken place after the fact, as in the case of asbestos.[1]

2 The development of technology to detect the presence of a hazardous material. It was after World War II that devices became available for detecting, measuring, and thereby regulating toxicity.

3 The development of epidemiology.[2] For example, some forms of cancer can take up to thirty years to develop after a very short exposure to a small quantity of asbestos. Epidemiology established a statistical relationship between these events and thus the probability that the one causes the other.

4 The development of the science of ecology, which takes into account not only the effects of a chemical on an insect but the consequences of those effects on plant life, other animals, and human beings. This approach began to be used in the evaluation of pesticides after Rachel Carson published *Silent Spring* (see Chapter 1).

5 The occurrence of a major disaster as a result of technological change. The thalidomide scandal in the 1950s is an example.

The problem with control triggered by reactions to events is that by the time the unfortunate consequences have been recognized, the technology is so much a part of the social and economic fabric of society that control is difficult (Collingridge 1980).

Over the years, various methods of controlling technology have been attempted, as illustrated in Table 1.

Table 1
Mechanisms for Controlling Technology

Category	Implications
No government intervention	Reliance on market forces
Criminal law	Legislation only as effective as the agencies responsible for implementing it
Civil law	More flexible but less satisfactory; puts responsibility on the individual who has been harmed to sue the person or organization responsible
Voluntary agreements	Not legally enforceable but even more flexible; can be amended whenever new evidence becomes available
Total government control	Complete transfer of decisions from private to public domain; sometimes involves nationalization of firms or industries responsible for negative effects of innovations

Source: Inspired by discussions of mechanisms for control in Coombs, Saviotti, and Walsh 1987.

The five categories of mechanisms for control of technology range from no official intervention to total government control. It must be noted that other structures often exist to ensure that laws or agreements are implemented: inspection programs, licensing authorities, or permission-granting bodies.

No intervention whatsoever often implies that a certain technology is so new that not much is known about it and its potential implications, or that it fits no existing legislation or regulatory category.

Criminal law puts legislation in place to cover the area in question: for example, death caused by noncompliance with safety standards. In civil law, responsibility rests on the person or persons harmed. Civil suits require money and legal aid that are often beyond the means of individuals and small groups. In addition, they require proof both that one party was harmed and that the other was negligent.

Voluntary agreements include indirect financial incentives to comply, such as an effluent tax levied on manufacturers for the discharge of waste material into the environment or an injury tax on employers. Voluntary agreements have been criticized because they can be considered an incentive to large and wealthy firms to avoid compliance: that is, it may be cheaper to pay the fines than to install safer equipment, proper ventilation, adequate protective clothing, and so on (Dalton 1979).

Characteristic of all the regulatory mechanisms in Table 1 is the assumption that a solution is possible. If it is determined that a product cannot be made without hazard to the user, the workers, or the environment, a controlling government can even ban the technology. Although such decisions are extremely rare, they have occurred. After the Swedish government decided that the use of asbestos was hazardous, all forms of the material were banned (Swedish National Board 1981).

The International Level
The OECD may have been the first forum of international cooperation for TA, but only by a narrow margin. In 1974 the European Community (EC) established a working and research group to formulate an action program for evaluation and methods; among other things, it was to determine the extent to which the EC should establish something similar to the OTA.

The group's report suggested establishing a European institute with approximately one hundred hired researchers, but that never happened. In 1978 the Council of Ministers of the EC decided to initiate an experimental program called Forecasting and Assessment in the Field of Science and Technology (FAST), which was implemented in 1979 by the appointment of a committee of six, including the program's administrator. The main aim of FAST was to contribute to the definition of long-term community research and development objectives and priorities, in order to formulate long-term, coherent science and technology policy (Bjoern-Andersen et al. 1982).

In identifying the fields within science and technology with which the EC would work, the committee identified three priority areas: biotechnology, work and employment, and information technology. The program also strove to encourage the establishment of an ad hoc system of collaboration in the form of informal and flexible networks between EC centers specializing in science forecasting and technology assessment. Its published studies were generally open to the public.[3]

Early on, FAST took up issues relevant to women. Recognizing that new technology was affecting various groups of workers in different ways, it financed a study that looked at new information technology and its effect on women's employment. By analyzing past and future labor market trends, this study confirmed that women would be a vulnerable group of workers in the future with regard to the introduction of new technology (Zmroczek and Henwood 1983).

Since large-scale technology is a product of the developed countries, it is not surprising that the TA movement originated and developed in these countries. It follows that the transfer of technology from developed to developing countries raises questions about the appropriateness of a given technology in another cultural context and reveals the need for modification and adaptation of TA. When TA is seen as the transfer of knowledge from one cultural context to another, it raises similar questions with regard to differences in social, economic, and political institutions and the implications for the application of this knowledge (Wad and Radnor 1984). I see the choices being made about technology as political choices. Therefore, I regard the TA process as an opportunity for developing countries to articulate their own values and confront them with the perceived costs (economic, social, and cultural) of various options. Viewing TA from this perspective minimizes the basic difference between developed and developing countries (Standke 1986).

National Examples

As a national consulting body, the OTA was the first example of TA to become institutionalized at government level. The United States is the only country that has organized TA directly under the legislative body.[4] The real significance of the OTA, however, has been that although it acts as a consultant to Congress, it can also initiate its own TA. Moreover, since it is directly linked to legislative power, it is independent of public administration in general.[5]

In the years that followed the establishment of the OTA, recommendations were made to set up similar structures in several European countries, but they were never followed.[6] Instead, various countries developed their own brands of TA based on what Jamison and Baark (1990) call the "cultural dimension of TA policy."

In the Federal Republic of Germany prior to German reunification, it was most often the civil services that administered TA. It was also here that major efforts were made to include TA in national research and technology policy (Teknologivurdering 1980). Several research and advisory institutions, independent of the universities and the technology service net, were established to carry out applied research in TA and the humanization of work, often with funds from the ministries of research and technology. This is an example of what I call "implicit" TA.[7] No funds are earmarked for TA per se because the ministry believes that it should be an integrated part of the general research program for the development of new technology. Other forms of implicit TA can also be found in Britain, France, and Sweden.

In the United Kingdom there has been no institutionalization of TA or any clearly recognizable TA discussions (Smits and Leyton 1988), but "attempts at technology assessment, by other names, are nevertheless made in practice" (Coombs, Saviotti, and Walsh 1987, 241). From the beginning it was felt that many TA functions were already being carried out by means of a task force approach: the occasional establishment of Royal Commissions to look at particular problems.

In France an attempt was made in the late 1970s to establish a French variant of the OTA. However, as was the case in Germany, the government feared that such a body would give parliament more strength, and therefore it blocked this and subsequent proposals (Smits and Leyton 1988). Since the early 1980s, however, the Socialist government's protechnology policy, adopted as a means of bringing France out of economic depression, has brought with it a great interest in TA activities designed to familiarize society with technology. Several institutions (rather than one central agency) have assumed responsibility for providing early-stage assessments.[8]

Rather than set up a special organization, Sweden decided that TA should be an integral part of all societal decision-making processes involving technology. In 1973 the Secretary for Future Studies under the Statsministeriet (the state department; in 1975 it came under the Riksdagen, or Swedish parliament) initiated such projects as investigations into "work life in Sweden," "resources and natural resources," and "energy and society." In 1978 the Arbejdslivscentrum was established as a research and advisory institute. Its governing board consists of representatives from the labor market partners (that is, the union and the employers' association), and its goal is to contribute to working life with applied research. That TA is an integrated and important element in many studies is the strength of the decentralized structure of TA in Sweden; the risk is that it may not make a coordinated contribution.

In the Netherlands, TA has been explicit rather than implicit. The Department for Research Policy and Strategic Studies under the Dutch Organization for Applied Scientific Research has played a major role in developing knowledge about TA. In 1987 an independent body established by the Ministry of Education emphasized the inclusion of TA in the decision-making process as well as the involvement of various social groups in the TA process (Dutch Ministry 1987).[9] The Netherlands has distinguished itself in Europe as a major contributor to the development of TA in general and MTA in particular.[10]

In Denmark too, TA has taken an explicit form. Originally the practice and domain of the private sector, it became an issue for debate in the mid-1970s, influenced by developments in the United States and the OECD. At this point, discussion was confined to small, closed circles of politicians and researchers (Danielsen 1990). The debate spread after 1980, when the Ministry of Industry's Council on Technology put out its first report on TA in Denmark. This report—dealing with broad issues such as "partisan research," the kinds of technology to be assessed, and the institutional placement of TA—met political resistance particularly from employer organizations (Remmen 1986), largely but not exclusively because of its emphasis on "partisan research."[11] It was not until 1986 that TA became institutionalized.

As the result of a long tradition of public involvement in political issues, Denmark has developed an approach to TA fundamentally different from that of most other countries. Danish TA is practiced as a combination of future research, evaluation research, and action research, the emphasis depending on whether it is part of the decision-making process or related to a concrete objective. One characteristic has been the debate on "alternative

TA," assessment of technological consequences that includes suggestions for a variety of solutions (Danielsen
1990). Denmark has what is called a "small-country approach to TA," in which almost all relevant actors are in
close interaction (Jamison and Baark 1990) and there is a
high degree of public participation.

Medical Technology Assessment
An important development in TA is the institutionalization of separate administrations dealing exclusively with
health care technology. Health care technology is defined
as comprising both the drugs, devices, and medical and
surgical procedures used in medical care, and the
organizational and support systems within which such
care is provided (STG 1987). In most countries, MTA
originally came under the same administration or ad hoc
research group as all other industrial technology. The
1980s saw the establishment of separate bodies and com-
mittees to carry out and/or administer MTA. One major
reason was the rapid advances made in the research and
development of health care technology, accompanied by
the increased dependency of the medical professions on
these advances: "Modern medicine has now evolved to a
point where diagnostic judgments based on subjective evidence—the patient's sensations and the physician's own
observations of the patient—are being supplanted by
judgments based on objective evidence, provided by laboratory procedures and by mechanical and electronic devices" (Reisner 1978, ix).
    Another factor was the influence of the medical pro-
fession in modern society.[12] Both nationally and internationally it was the medical profession that established
and headed MTA initiatives. Separating MTA from TA in
general and ensuring that physicians have a leading role
in determining MTA policy can be seen as a form of self-
regulation. This development resulted in the introduction

of medical doctors to the traditional team of active technology assessors: engineers, technicians, and economists.

A contributing if not the major cause of the sudden interest in MTA in the 1980s was a general international trend: the proportion of the gross national product (GNP) going to health care had more than doubled since the 1950s (Brorsson and Wall 1985). In the mid-1980s, health care costs as a percentage of GNP had reached 6.2 percent in the United Kingdom, 6.6 percent in Denmark, 9.6 percent in Sweden, and 10.8 percent in the United States (OECD 1985). Other economic factors included the huge financial interests of the medico-technology industry and the active interest of third-party payers.[13]

Initially, international organizations also played a role in organizing MTA. A World Health Organization (WHO) program on health care technology promised to assist countries that wanted to improve their regulatory systems for drugs and medical devices (Institute of Medicine 1985).[14]

Among national projects, the STG (Commission on Future Health Care Technology) functioned in the Netherlands from 1985 to 1987.[15] Its purpose was to assist in long-term health planning, with emphasis on cardiovascular disease, cancer, aging, and lifestyles as issues of importance to the future health of the Dutch population.

The need for a more comprehensive and widespread MTA in Denmark was established in 1982 in a formal statement by the Ministry of the Interior. In 1983 a special committee at the National Board of Health was made responsible for future activity in this area. The committee's goal was threefold: to follow the development of medical technology, to introduce the concept of MTA into the health care sector, and to initiate concrete projects. Although the mandate was to establish a committee of "generalists," the majority of members were physicians.

In 1988 the Swedish Council on Technology Assessment in Health Care was established as an independent

agency within the Secretariat of the Swedish Government.[16] This was prompted by a proposal from a task force
that had earlier been charged by the Ministry of Health
and Social Affairs to study the need for national coordination of MTA. The task force was subsequently asked to
define the scope of MTA and to suggest how activities at
the national level should be organized (IJTAHC 1989).
There have been similar developments in Australia and
elsewhere.[17]

Unlike other countries, France at present has virtually
no systematic assessment strategy for current medical
technology or practice. One reason is that TA in France
has generally been linked to regional development. The
piecemeal assessment that does exist is largely the result
of isolated efforts in the research sector, particularly by
the Institut National de la Santé et de la Recherche Medi-
cale (INSERM) (IJTAHC 1989).

In both Western Europe and the United States, there
is an obvious trend toward an increase in the number of
institutes, national research councils, and individuals
who are involved in MTA. This can be seen in part as a
result of public pressure, social movements, and consumer consciousness.[18]

Non-Institutionalized TA
The concern and influence of special interest groups, especially pressure groups, have been increasing, and the
general attitude has become critical. "Neither technology
nor social systems are static, and changes in both of them
can create conflicts of interest that no present institution
is capable of handling. Thus many new pressure groups
have become increasingly prominent in the political systems of western countries, and a number of them have
been concerned with issues with a strong technological
dimension" (Coombs, Saviotti, and Walsh 1987, 265). The
newer groups include various regional and national con-

sumer organizations as well as labor unions, which have become increasingly critical of new technology.

A special interest group usually chooses to concern itself with one single issue or a range of related issues in order to achieve the greatest impact. Some groups have attempted to inform companies, the government, and the general public about the rate, direction, and consequences of technological change—particularly when market mechanisms and government policy have failed to satisfy a substantial sector of public opinion (Coombs, Saviotti, and Walsh 1987).

Labor unions continue to challenge the organizational and occupational health hazards of technology, often by negotiating technology agreements with employers. In the Federal Republic of Germany the trade unions were successful in pressuring the government to form a program for the improvement of working conditions, organized within a state technology stimulation program (Smits and Leyten 1988). One of the few kinds of pressure groups with available funds, trade unions in some countries now have their own research departments whose job is to supply union negotiators with technical, economic, and other information as an alternative to that made available by employers. Issues include health and safety at work, and the effects of new technology on job availability, work organization, and skills. Unions can often afford to hire outside experts to supply them with information as well. In Denmark there is even an official collaboration between academics and trade unions, which is sponsored by public funds.

The environmental movement became a significant voice in the 1970s. Initially, it was composed of various smaller pressure groups whose basic concerns were the obvious threats to human existence. The movement has since turned from outright rejection of modern technology to more optimistic promotion of "alternative" concepts of technology (Cramer, Eyerman, and Jamison

1987). In the United States, environmentalists ran a successful campaign to remove lead from gasoline. In Denmark, the government abandoned plans for a nuclear program as the result of the environmental movement's active and much publicized opposition. In some countries, ecology groups have become so political that their beliefs have formed the basis for political parties, such as the Green parties that have emerged in Europe and Scandinavia.

Pressure groups do not always have all the technical information they need, nor the funds to buy it, to plead their case against a certain development. They must often search for data outside their own sphere of expertise, and access to such data is a problem in many countries. The American Freedom of Information Act allows the public access to government archives (excluding of course, "top secret" files), often including the plans and specifications of new developments within industry. This is not the case in most other countries, however. The British government, for example, can suppress information about a government-sponsored project for as long as it chooses. Not only is there no freedom-of-information act, but the United Kingdom has a government secrets and confidentiality act that permits it to withhold scientific material and data from the public (Doyal et al. 1983). Consequently, British researchers must often request information from the United States about products and drugs that are sold and even sometimes manufactured in the United Kingdom.

In the Netherlands as well as in Denmark, "science shops" have been established at some of the universities to consider the problems of technology that confront community groups or trade unions. Sometimes staff members with the appropriate expertise are commissioned to do the necessary research, which is often paid for with university funds.

Pressure groups have gained in both influence and expertise over the years and are becoming a valuable information resource for TA, especially in the area of health care technology.

Consumer Health Issues

Government-established consumer protection organizations in one form or another existed as far back as the nineteenth century. Nongovernmental consumer groups have existed even longer. It was following World War II, however, that a grassroots health care movement took shape. It can be seen as the health care users' protest against their perceived powerlessness and secondary role within the established system. They began questioning the basic precepts of the system and its dependence on a "medical model" of health (Oakley and Houd 1990).

Medical patient consumerism began in the 1960s. Consumer concern over health issues appeared as a demand for better health information in the mid-1970s and continued to grow throughout the 1980s. In a nationwide American survey on consumers' views about barriers to better health (Harris 1978), respondents were asked what they regarded as the top three industries to which the consumer movement should pay particular attention. From a list of twenty-five industries, survey participants chose hospitals, the medical profession, and food manufacturers.

Once dismissed as a fad, medical consumerism has developed into a legitimate and important social movement. The reasons include the rising cost of health care, new public awareness of individual responsibility for health care decision-making, and the widespread failure of health professionals to satisfy adequately the information needs of consumers (Rees 1982). Another contributing factor has been the increase in the incidence of chronic disease, which requires patients to become more knowledgeable about their illness than is essential for

those with acute disorders, since they have the disease
longer and are more experienced with treatment.
Health information services have been established in
several European countries as well as in the United
States. Implicit in this movement's agenda is concern for
the use and development of health care technology. The
proliferation of new medical technology creates more
treatment options. As a result of increasing malpractice
litigation, doctors now call on patients to take more responsibility in the decision-making process, often placing
individual patients in a role they are unprepared for.

The most influential health-related pressure groups in
many countries, particularly in the United Kingdom and
the United States, have been patients' associations. These
groups focus on a particular disease or class of disease
such as heart problems or arthritis. Many such associations have been accumulating knowledge in their fields
for years and retain expert advisers who represent their
profession and have access to other experts. Members use
a variety of methods to promote their interests, including
the lobbying of ministers, parliaments, and Congress
(CSS 1982). It is worth noting that patients' organizations
are often headed (or at any rate greatly influenced) by
members of the medical profession, who have a vested interest in gaining access to expensive medical technology
(CSS 1982), as well as in furthering their own careers.[19]

Third-party payers have played a central role in initiating TA projects in the health care sector.[20] The enormous costs associated with new medical technology have
thrust them into a dominant role in the development, diffusion, and adoption of new technology. All these payers
need comprehensive information related to established,
new, and future technologies, yet each group also wants
to be in control of its own decisions. While they all seek
more and better information, they are also competing
with one another and have different needs. No single
group can sponsor a comprehensive program of TA by it-

self, but each is fearful of delegating responsibility and losing control of its own policies and programs. Furthermore, no single group wishes to fund the development of new technology without a high degree of certainty that the findings will be directly applicable in solving the particular problems it faces.

The Women's Health Movement

An original area of focus for the organized movement of health care users was a critique of perinatal care, motivated by the use of high-tech methods and high-cost solutions to problems (Oakley and Houd 1990). The women's health movement, evolving from the women's movement, began in the early 1970s. It has been activist in orientation but has extensive grounding in research and education.[21]

Contributing factors to the growth of this movement were perceived inadequacies in available health care and the power imbalance in society affecting women's health (Ratcliff 1989). One of the earliest activities of the women's liberation movement in the 1970s was a critique of established medical practices and the ways in which changing health care technology can affect the relationship between women and health. The feminist interest in health and health care has obvious causes: first, women are the most frequent users of medical services; second, they form the majority of health workers.

In the 1970s the struggle for control over women's bodies focused on birth control and abortion: that is, the right *not* to have a child (Rose 1987). Issues related to human reproduction have since been a major though not exclusive focus of interest. Groups concerned with pregnancy and childbirth (and not women's groups exclusively) began questioning the medicalization of birth—that is, the medical profession's increasing use of high-tech diagnostic and treatment techniques such as electronic fetal monitoring during normal deliveries—as well as the control of women's fertility in general (Doyal, Kickbusch, and Morgall 1984).[22]

Although reproductive technology has always been a major concern of feminists, some women's groups have been shedding their grassroots image and becoming more focused and strategic in their approach. This has resulted in their taking stronger stands on issues of technology, in many cases rejecting its use outright. According to some popular perceptions, either one accepts all emerging technological innovations or one is considered anti-technology. This is particularly true in the area of medical technology, where being anti-technology is equated with being anti-health and anti-cure.

The out-and-out rejection of some technology by the women's health movement can be seen as a reaction to several disasters involving various forms of reproductive technology: that is, birth control pills, thalidomide, DES (diethylstilbestrol).[23] The thalidomide scandal provides an insight into issues considered important by the women's health movement; it illustrates

> the potential consequences of a style of medical practice quick to intervene with drugs and other forms of technology in an environment where profit can outweigh human concern, and the particularly exploitive and harmful consequences for women who have little voice or direct power over their health care. It illustrates why the combined effects of overzealous medical intervention and the subordinate position of women in society constitute a key theme in the feminist critique of medicine. [Zimmerman 1987, 446]

Work-related issues have also been a concern of the women's health movement. Numerous studies were carried out in the 1970s and 1980s on occupational health problems in women-dominated employment sectors: for example, the clerical sector (Morgall 1981b), including the relationship between new office technology and health hazards (Morgall 1982f). Other activities taken up in the 1970s addressed issues of public access to health services, as well as access to and the quality of health information. Feminists criticized the latter for not being sufficiently critical or in the best interests of women.[24]

The strategies used to organize the women's health movement were based primarily on two methods employed in the women's movement: self-help groups, and political action organizations (Zimmerman 1987). Self-help groups can be categorized roughly as the health equivalent of the feminist consciousness-raising groups of the late 1960s and early 1970s. They began in the 1970s as a way for women to learn about themselves through mutual discussion and the sharing of information. The structure provided by these self-help initiatives can be seen as making three contributions: nonhierarchical organization and equal participation among members, a new approach to available knowledge about women's bodies and health, and the direct provision of health care services to women by women (Zimmerman 1987).

In the mid-1980s, while consumer health information services were being established in countries on both sides of the Atlantic, the women's health movement set up "documentation centers" to deal specifically with women's health issues (Morgall 1984a). Their purpose was to create small, community-based centers to meet the specific health information needs of local women and to present unbiased health information and education materials: that is, materials exposing the conflicts and contradictions found in the medical literature.

The popularity of participating in self-help in the women's health movement had declined by the early 1980s. Zimmerman (1987) attributes the decline to several factors, including the attempt of organized medicine to co-opt self-help by endorsing health education, prevention, and the individual's increased responsibility for her or his health. Through the activities of its political action organizations, however, the women's health movement has gone on to work for political, legal, and institutional changes. Early examples can be found in the struggle for legal abortion and the fights to shed public light on the use of thalidomide and DES.

A more recent concern is with the development and application of reproductive technology, as reflected in the work of FINRRAGE. Organized in 1984, the Feminist International Network of Resistance to Reproductive and Genetic Engineering believes that "externalization of conception and gestation facilitates manipulation and eugenic control" and that reproductive technology uses biology to solve social and political problems created by exploitive conditions (Solomon 1989). FINRRAGE represents a radical feminist perspective. It sees reproductive technology as inextricably linked to genetic engineering and eugenics. Not all feminists agree with this point of view; its critics dispute what they call FINRRAGE's "monolithic male conspiracy theory." Other feminist perspectives have focused instead on such issues as the ambivalent influence of these technologies on women's lives, women's rights with regard to choice and to access, the potential for abuse of technologies, and the need for a political democratic control over their use.[25]

Summary
This chapter has presented examples of institutionalized and non-institutionalized TA as they exist today. Certain preconditions are likely to lead to consideration of government control of technology. Government options range from no control at all to total control or even an outright ban on the technology in question.

The desire of most European countries to link TA to the legislative body has not been realized; in most cases of governmental organization, it has come under the central administration. Each country has had its own method of establishing TA, either by making it implicit in all science and technology research or by making it an explicit activity with its own budget.

The noticeable exception in the organization of TA is in health care technology. In many countries MTA has established itself independently of other forms of TA, most often under the control of physicians. One reason is the desire to control public spending in health care, which, as a percentage of GNP, has more than doubled since the 1950s. Other factors—rapid advances in the development of sophisticated health care technology, the high price of medical equipment, the huge investments and economic interests of the medico-technology industry—have combined with an increased dependency on technology by the medical profession to make assessment a necessary tool in creating health care policy.

Pressure groups have become increasingly critical of technological development, and their interest in and influence on TA is on the rise, as can be seen in the area of consumer health issues. Since the early 1970s the women's health movement has been addressing issues concerning the effects of technology on the relationship between women and health.

3

Methods and Their Limitations

Although numerous methods are used to assess technology, there are two primary forms: retroactive and proactive. Retroactive assessment looks back on the application of a given technology in order to evaluate its effects and recommend future applications. It is an assessment of an already disseminated technology. Proactive assessment begins with a "need" or a "problem," which is described and evaluated. The object is to initiate a process that will help solve the problem or meet the need. If it is decided that the best solution is a technological one, then requirements for that technology can be determined in advance.

Proactive research has a long tradition in industry, where the motivation is economic: "There has been an inclination to search for better economic results by foreseeing obstacles to technological innovation beforehand" (OECD 1983, 12). Proactive assessment is less common outside industry, in the social or health care sectors for example.[1] Proactive research necessitates a general policy analysis based on well-thought-out societal needs, an approach that has unfortunately been nonexistent in most countries. An OECD overview published in 1983, however, did emphasize that after a period of being influenced by a backward-looking (reactive) criticism, TA was finally developing as a forward-looking (proactive) discipline.

A "constructive approach" to TA has been evolving which attempts to bring technology policy into the earliest stages of technological development. Whereas traditional TA focused on external effects and the choice between different technologies, constructive TA shifts the attention to the steering of the internal development of technology (Remmen 1991). Sometimes referred to as interactive or "strategic TA," it is now being tried by industry in some countries, notably Japan.[2]

Many methods of TA developed during phase one, especially in the United States. Mathematical methods and techniques developed at this time were promoted as means of dealing with the great number of variables as well as the high level of ambiguity inherent in TA research (Berg and Michael 1978). These procedures proved to be very limited, however.

Other methods have sought to assess costs versus benefits, as well as to develop an overview of precisely which means are relevant to a given goal. For example, among techniques for preserving food are the addition of preservatives and airtight packaging. In deciding which to use, the difference in approach between a narrow assessment (common in phase one) and a broader-based assessment (introduced in phase two) is that in the latter it is not enough to know that there are two equally efficient ways to preserve food. A broad analysis questions more than efficiency. An economic analysis would ask, which way is cheaper? An ecological analysis would ask, does the process or the finished product disturb the food chain or pollute the environment? A health analysis would ask, does the process introduce health hazards? A labor market analysis would ask, does either process create or eliminate jobs? A feminist analysis would ask, what are the implications (if any) for women? Does this process or finished product affect their role in the work-place or at home, or their health?

TA is seen as the means of determining the procedure that best serves the goal. And such a determination is dependent not only on whether the product, system, or process has the ability to fulfill a given function but also on whether it promotes (or hinders) other activities that the interested parties are committed to support or have promised to undertake.

This chapter describes the most frequently used methods of assessment. I have selected methods commonly used for assessing emerging technology in general and, in most cases, emerging medical technology as well. My treatment excludes those methods of a purely technical nature, as they have no relevance to the purpose of this study other than to demonstrate that they alone are not enough.

Economic Analysis

Economic interests have always been a major consideration in technological development. Since TA originally developed in industry and later became one of the main concerns of policy-makers, it is not surprising to find that economic analysis has been one of the most frequently used methods. Economic analyses are essentially concerned with how to use resources in ways that get the best value from them. Such considerations involve the comparison of various options. In fact, analyses that disclose the relationship between expected performance and monetary costs are a traditional part of all engineering planning and design (Starr 1972).

The most frequently used economic assessments have been cost-benefit analysis (CBA) and cost-effectiveness analysis (CEA). Historically, the first demand for CBA came from public administrations. It is an analytical technique that compares the costs of a technology with the resultant benefits, with costs and benefits both expressed by the same measure, which is nearly always monetary. Cost-benefit analysis was developed for the purpose of making it possible to decide on the optimum allocation of resources between competing demands for government expenditure (in cases of nonpriced services), to improve knowledge of the relationship between resources used and results achieved. Analyzing the costs of manufacturing a product or performing a service and comparing those costs with the user's willingness to pay provide a basis for deciding how to allocate resources. CBA seeks to answer these questions: Does using this technology pay off? Is this technology worth developing and introducing into the workplace (or into health care services, or other programs)?

Cost-effectiveness analysis (CEA) is an analytical technique that compares the costs of a project with the resultant benefits but expresses them by different measures: costs are usually expressed in monetary terms, whereas benefits (effectiveness) are expressed in terms such as "accidents avoided," "lives saved" (STG 1987). CEA seeks to find the most effective technique or technology for using given resources. It can assist, for example, in making decisions about techniques for health care delivery.

The limitations of economic analysis often derive from the fact that it tends to use methods that are implicitly linked to theory, but it makes no reference to theory. One explanation is that these methods are often used by people who are not economists and are not even aware of the theoretical basis.

> Problems do arise in the application of these techniques [CBA and CEA] which cannot always be fully overcome—problems of data availability, cost and benefit measurement, lack of ideal output measures, and so on. Nonetheless it is important that, if the use of these techniques is to grow in the health service and be seen to be useful, more and more health-service staff and decision-makers should

be familiar with the theory and concepts underlying the techniques. Indeed it can be argued that the growth in the usage of the term "cost-benefit" has been much more rapid than the growth of understanding of cost-benefit analysis. Unless this is corrected there is grave danger that the usefulness of cost-benefit analysis will not be fully appreciated. [Mooney, Russell, and Weir 1980, 58]

Cost-benefit analysis is theoretically based within that branch of economic theory called new welfare economics or Paretian welfare economics (after the Swiss-Italian economist and sociologist Vilfredo Pareto). This branch has its roots in classical economics and is concerned with decisions about what conditions in the economy will maximize the social welfare under given resource restrictions. CBA was developed for the purpose of making it possible to improve knowledge of the relationship between resources and results, especially in the case of nonpriced goods. One problem in welfare economics theory is how to evaluate changes in social welfare and how to choose criteria for evaluation. One method is the so-called Pareto-criterion: an obtainable condition that can make conditions better for one actor without making them worse for another. This criterion is both weak and restrictive—weak because an efficient resource allocation in economics could be made endless by applying the criterion to a number of possible methods of distributing goods; restrictive because very few projects do not include the worsening of conditions for one or several actors. The weakness of the method itself is that CBA cannot tell whether the objective is worth achieving or how far one should push the effort. These questions require further data, analysis, and value judgments.

The widening gap between available resources and the increasing demand for services and goods, along with the recognition of various interest groups, has created a growing concern about CBA's usefulness as a decision-making tool.

The content of a CBA is not standardized. The question as to which and how many criteria should be included in an analysis can only be answered in very general terms: as many as possible to ensure that no relevant effects are overlooked. This principle of CBA has not, however, always been followed in practice. It has been far more often the case that *an effect has been included or omitted according to whether or not it could be quantified.* [Dinkel 1985, 327; emphasis added]

Because it is difficult if not impossible to quantify human and social costs, they are seldom included in the equation. Instead, technical benefits are assessed against the costs of correcting, through the use of technology, any problems that arise: an example of the "technological fix," the belief that a problem created by technology can be solved by technology.

Against the background of changing goals in policy-making, the use of CBA is becoming increasingly more questionable, particularly in the health care sector: "A CBA graduated in accordance with the interest groups involved *offers the decision maker* (e.g., government authorities or other third-party payers) *the opportunity to recognize areas of potential resistance* in the health service system to a new technology. By means of appropriate measures, for example by introducing incentives or prohibitions, the decision maker can ensure that the potential for cost savings is in fact realized" (Dinkel 1985, 327; emphasis added). This quotation highlights what I see as the most serious threat to a critical TA analysis: knowledge interests that seek to quantify and control human and social conditions and to *avoid* conflict can employ methods to detect potential resistance rather than analyze the reasons for it. The simple but important thinking underlying the CBA approach is that we should do only those things the benefits of which are greater than the costs, and stop doing those things for which this is not the case (Mooney, Russell, and Weir 1980).

In contrast to CBA, cost-effectiveness analysis is a clearly atheoretical method and can be classified as mere technique. CEA is not explicitly tied to economic theory; it was developed in response to a need for solving practical problems whose goal and desired effect were given and the task was to achieve the goal at the lowest possible cost (Nyemark 1989). CEA in itself provides no assistance in deciding whether or not to pursue a particular policy, or how much of a particular policy to pursue.

The OTA (1980) has emphasized that although CEA and CBA can improve decision-making by assessing not only whether a given technology is effective but also whether it is worth the cost, they should not serve as the sole or primary determinants of a health care decision.

Systems Analysis
Early methods of TA were closely linked to the development of technology, which at that time was primarily a concern with technique (as opposed to a concern for solving social problems): for example, "the race to the moon" (Braendgaard 1983). Methods of assessing goals and means were developed which could be expressed in unequivocal functional demands. In this way, if the assessment was successful, neither the technical experts nor the decision-makers would have any basis for doubt.

In early attempts to broaden TA, by far the most preferred method was systems analysis: the process of studying an activity or procedure by defining its aims and purposes in order to find the operations and procedures to accomplish them most efficiently and economically. A systems study asks, how and why does this system as a whole function as it does? (Patton 1990).

The systems approach is based on the idea that the dispassionate, clear mind of the scientist can aid in decision-making. It was originally applied by the Allied forces in the form of operational research during the Battle of

Britain (1940–41) to make their bombings of the Nazis more efficient. Following the success in the United Kingdom and United States of these specially convened scientific teams in assisting the military effort, there was a rush after the war to apply the method to various nonmilitary problems: industry in particular, production, marketing, and finance (Churchman 1968). The methodology became the stock in trade of various U.S. think tanks such as the Rand Corporation. According to Hoos (1982), the historical military origin of systems techniques was often cited as proof of their prowess. Decision-makers in industry and in government began to see the possible usefulness of this approach, based on a belief "that people who are well trained in the design of complex hardware systems such as space missiles should be able to apply their thinking to the critical decision-making problems of the state" (Churchman 1968, x).

A vast body of literature has developed about systems theory and systems research. Much of it is extremely quantitative and involves complex computer applications and simulations (Patton 1990). Braendgaard (1983) refers to systems analysis as one of the most "ambitious leadership models for society." Widespread in the 1960s and early 1970s, it was closely associated with the very origins of TA—so much so that it was incorporated into an early OECD definition of TA: "Technology assessment is a systems analysis approach to providing a whole conceptual framework, complete both in scope and time, for decisions about the appropriate utilization of technology for social purposes" (Hetman 1973).

Like other methods, this one has its limitations. Systems analysis has its origins in operations research and its theoretical roots in systems theory. Operations research applied scientific methods to the management and administration of organized military, governmental, commercial, and industrial systems and was designed to deal with problems that have less than clearly defined objectives, including a variety of economic and social problems. Systems theory is an attempt to supply systematic reasoning to the coordination of complex systems and the structuring of complex problems. It is a way of thinking that emphasizes the technical side of problems over their social and political dimensions. In this theoretical approach, a study of any given society looks at how its various parts or institutions combine to give that society continuity over time. In sociology, this is referred to as the functionalist viewpoint, which, along with functionalist theories, is often seen as unduly conservative because of its stress on stability rather than change. The basic idea is that political systems can be seen as analogues to operating mechanical systems with feedback loops and clear goals.

"Systems analysis was adapted as one of the subdisciplines of the general systems theory movement" (Churchman 1968, 200). It was seen as an attempt to spread the responsibility for rational planning and decision-making by demonstrating that individuals, corporations, and public industries were all interrelated (Baram 1973). It has been criticized, however, for being noncritical in its approach (Hoos 1982), and as a method used in TA it risks treating technical and social issues as equally valid:

> Although systems theory offers a holistic approach to the study of social problems, the social imagery involved is no less abstract than that which is associated with a technological world-view. A mechanistic analogy is adopted to explain order, for individuals are described as objects or parts, human action is defined as energy, and interpersonal harmony is viewed as equilibrium. . . . Consistent with technological rationality, the use of systems theory objectified society and transformed it into a self-equilibrating system. Systems theory is insufficient to render technology socially responsible, since human action is portrayed in a manner consistent with the aims of technological rationality. Again, primacy for judging human behavior is given to technical

criteria. All other alternatives are disregarded, thereby allowing the dominance of technological rationality to go unchallenged. [Murphy 1987, 70–71]

As Murphy argues, an understanding of the "technological worldview" is necessary before technology (and TA) can have a social meaning. Holistic approaches exist in the critical and the feminist literature, but contrary to systems analysis, they are *not* based on mechanistic models (see Part II).

Given their respective limitations, systems analysis and economic analysis gradually gave way to a more general policy analysis approach, which meant developing other methods.

Risk Assessment

If one method of controlling a technology is to ban its development or dissemination, an alternative is to accept the existence of risk and to measure it explicitly.

Risk is expressed in terms of the damage that would be done if a particular event occurred, multiplied by the probability of that event's occurring (CSS 1977).[3] Risk assessment is complicated by the fact that certain technological changes benefit some people but generate costs or potential costs for others. Sometimes risks and benefits are experienced by the same person. A system of tradeoffs has to be established: one accepts a certain level of risk in exchange for a benefit.

There are national cultural differences in approaches to risk assessment. In studying risk assessment and road safety, for example, Irwin (1985) found that consumer groups in the United States demand corporate responsibility for product safety. As a result of the American passion for litigation, the major advances in motor vehicle safety have been in occupant protection. In the United Kingdom, the emphasis has been on traffic engineering:

that is, maximizing safety through improved lighting, signs, and road surfaces.

Like systems analysis, risk assessment has its origins in operational research. Coombs, Saviotti, and Walsh (1987) conclude that risk assessment is *not* a scientific precursor to regulatory policy but is itself part of the process that shapes policy.

There are several problems with risk assessment, of which vested interest and public access to knowledge are but two. In the matter of vested interest, the status of scientific knowledge may challenge public costs when set against private benefit. The degree of benefit and risk can vary with the individual, however, apart from any conflict of interest. For example, with birth control pills, some people would argue that the benefits of not conceiving justify the risk of side effects. Sometimes, the susceptibility to side effects varies with circumstances, for example, smokers over thirty-five years old are at higher risk. Individual acceptance of risk varies not only with benefits but also with other circumstances that determine the nature and immediacy of the risk. During periods of high unemployment, workers may find themselves weighing potential risks to their health against unemployment (Iversen 1990), and in many countries the immediate certainty of unemployment is considered worse than the possibility of disease.

The major problem facing risk assessment is that the benefits and risks may affect different people or groups. For example, a person may suffer ill health from the pollution of a local factory *without* receiving the benefit of employment there. Here assessment of risk and the establishment of regulation become a matter of achieving an acceptable balance between public cost and private benefit.

Public tolerance of acceptable risk varies a great deal and must be taken into account. Although nuclear power generators have been responsible for few accidents, the risk for potential deaths is higher than with other energy forms: In air travel there are fewer accidents but more deaths per accident; in private motor travel, the most accidents but fewer deaths.

Public access to knowledge or information is an important factor in risk analysis. There are two sides: people may be less likely to accept risks when they feel they lack information, but not knowing the risks can result in an "ignorance is bliss" approach. Problems resulting from lack of information can occur either because knowledge does not exist or because people do not have or are unaware of how to get access to existing knowledge.

The Controlled Clinical Trial

With the introduction of more efficient medical therapies in the 1940s and 1950s—including drugs, preparations, and equipment—doctors realized the importance of evaluating their effectiveness. This led to the general introduction of the controlled clinical trial (CCT), which compares the new treatment under evaluation either with a placebo or with the previous standard treatment. If possible, testing is done on a double-blind basis, where neither the patient nor the doctor knows at the time whether the test treatment or the control is being administered.

The CCT is the method most commonly used to examine the effects on health of specific technological medical intervention. The advantages of CCTs are that they provide systematic documented information about the appropriateness of medical technology. They are the dominant method of assessing pharmaceuticals prior to licensing and marketing in the Western world. But because the CCT is being adopted as a major evaluation tool in many countries lacking other appropriate methods, it is important that a distinction be made between CCTs and TA.

Technological assessment is defined as having broad concerns related to technological change as well as to health outcome, and as a form of policy analysis. The CCT is merely a method, a method with many limitations.

Its disadvantages are many. The CCT is definitely a method born of theory and related to research tradition, in this case to what is known as the "medical model" (see Part II). But like cost-benefit analysis, it is often used by people who are unaware of its theoretical roots, and it is therefore open to abuse. Such abuses have international implications. For one thing, pharmaceutical companies often find it is easier (and cheaper) to carry out CCTs (experiments on humans) in countries where there is little or no controlling legislation; often these are developing countries. For another, the results of the CCTs are frequently applied to countries other than the one where the tests were performed.

In practice, CCTs are time-consuming and very expensive. The sample size is often too small, making it impossible to draw inferences about narrowly defined groups of patients, and thus not well designed from a scientific point of view. The results are often gross generalizations, so one must be cautious in applying them. Moreover, CCTs are often done under "ideal" circumstances—that is, with the best medical personnel and in the best hospitals—rather than under more usual conditions. Then there are what Hansen and Launsoe (1987) call problems that are "out of reach of CCT": the placebo effect, noncompliance, unknown and unexpected (adverse) effects. Last but not least, CCTs seldom address social or policy issues; in fact, they are often done too late in the development and diffusion of the technology to be of any help in making policy decisions. They concentrate instead on the interests of researchers and clinicians and apply only biological methods. They *could* be used in combination with other measures but seldom are, as pointed out in my discussion of a feminist approach to MTA (Part II).

Synthesis Methods

Synthesis methods became increasingly popular in the 1970s and 1980s, particularly in MTA. Synthesis is the compilation and evaluation of available knowledge. Two motives for synthesis analysis can be observed. One is scientific and aims at establishing the direction of the research; the other attempts to extract applicable information from a wealth of different studies. The results can be used either to examine critically the state of the art of a given field or to create a basis for policy discussion with a view to stimulating interest in the field. Syntheses are considered important in controversial areas, where they can help develop a consensus concerning which results can be aggregated and which questions can be answered using available knowledge (Brorsson and Wall 1985).

Synthesis methods have been a basic tool in the OTA model (Banta, Behney, and Willems 1981), which uses a process of analyzing, synthesizing, and reanalyzing. The result is an assessment that under ideal conditions should be ongoing. The method for synthesis developed and promoted by the OTA collects existing but unrelated information, analyzes it, and then draws conclusions. This is all done without the necessity for collecting new data.

There are two major approaches to synthesis analysis. One is through literature reviews and meta-analysis; the other, through the group processes so often used today. Meta-analysis is otherwise known as the "analysis of analyses." It is performed by taking the numeric results from each individual study and aggregating them. Meta-analysis makes it possible to determine the average effect of a technology (expressed in standard units) and how the effect varies within the groups studied.

Group-process methods became popular in phase two, when there was a strong desire to involve the public in assessment. Frequently used group-process methods include the *Delphi Technique*, named for the Oracle at Delphi, which was thought to predict the future. Developed for the U.S. military in the early 1950s, it attempts to integrate expert opinion about the future in order to predict national defense needs and the consequences of policies and trends. By employing written questionnaires with cycles of feedback, it is a tool for developing the consensus of experts without a meeting of the participants.

Consensus development conferences, as used in the United States, can be compared to court proceedings. After hearing testimony from selected experts in a two-day meeting, a consensus panel is asked to draft a statement concerning the appropriate conditions for use of the technology in question. This consensus statement is then widely distributed to policy-makers, professionals, the media, and the public.

Public inquiries invite individuals in large numbers to comment on technological issues (such as nuclear power) via the media, radio phone-ins, and public meetings. Such inquiries are one method by which the public may alter decisions with which it does not agree.

Social experiments involve the public by introducing technology experimentally in order to assess the qualitative consequences for everyday life, social relations, and the like. They are related to the planning, design, and implementation of innovative intervention programs; the novel character of the independent or input variables are the grounds for designating an activity an "experiment." The term implies close control over an intervention, and often an attempt is made to minimize contaminating influences on outcomes.

Future workshops, developed in the Federal Republic of Germany, gather multidisciplinary groups (including decision-makers) and over a three-day period ask them to define, confront, and overcome barriers to the "ideal" conditions under which a given technology should be used.

The Delphi Technique is an intellectual activity, as are consensus conferences (which have the added purpose of being planned media events). If either of these activities were to be theoretically grounded (though reference to theory is rarely made), they would be linked to one of the central issues of sociology: the question of how social order is established and preserved. Social theory on this issue can be divided into arguments that coercion is the basis of social order (conflict theories), and arguments that some degree of general consensus over values and norms provides the crucial basis of societies (consensus theories). Seen within a larger theoretical framework, these methods obviously belong within consensus theory in that they *assume* the possibility of consensus and discourage conflict.

It is the major criticism of consensus conferences that conflicts are covered up and not at all encouraged. Some critics refer to the consensus statement presented on the last day of the conference as a document reflecting the "lowest common denominator" (Koch and Morgall 1987). Such conferences have been criticized by feminists primarily because they are heavily weighted with professionals, thereby forcing a focus on technical rather than social and human issues. The consequences in matters of particular concern for women, such as treatment of breast cancer or the use of reproductive technology, are not always optimal. Finally, demanding consensus eliminates the option to reject a technology outright.

Literature review, another so-called method, is really only a technique. Of course, once the research question is formulated, the review becomes linked to a theory and itself becomes selective. It is not uncommon, however, to find literature reviews used in TA with no attempt to put the work within a theoretical framework. Meta-analysis, based on literature reviews, relies on numeric equations of specified variables: for example, the criteria for disease. It is used more and more often, particularly as the result of the increasingly widespread use of computers. The biggest disadvantage is that the criteria for the variables represented in numeric form often do not meet the same criteria in all studies, making the validity of the aggregate questionable. The accuracy of the results is limited by the accuracy of the data the analysis employs. A major limitation of both literature reviews and meta-analysis is that they may be premature; that is, not all the evidence has yet been put forward in the literature. In the case of MTA, the literature is based on CCTs, which at best can give a "clinical" evaluation that in no way takes psychological and social needs into account.

One method by which the public can influence technological development is public inquiry, a kind of complaints procedure. In the early 1970s large numbers of persons were invited to comment on technological issues such as nuclear power in the former Federal Republic of Germany, Sweden, and Denmark. Public inquiries are limited in scope, however, and infrequent. Moreover, "most members of the public, even if they feel very strongly about an issue, do not feel they have the time or the expertise to present evidence at a public enquiry, or the resources to commission an expert to do it for them" (Coombs, Saviotti, and Walsh 1987, 258).

Danish experience in involving the public through social experiments shows that the consequences of, for example, information technologies are first and foremost within humanistic areas such as psychology, communication, culture, aesthetics, and ethics (Remmen 1986). To understand these consequences, it is not enough to do experiments; qualitative analysis methods must be developed. A major criticism of social experiments is that there is no guarantee that the results cannot be used as an advanced form of promoting new technology, or by the government to promote and introduce its plans for the future (Müller, Remmen, and Christensen 1986). Advanced reproductive technology, for example, usually begins with an "experimental status" and quietly becomes routine procedure without so much as a public debate.

Future workshops are the only TA method from the foregoing selection that is both theoretically based and critical, and capable of addressing group-specific problems. The theoretical roots of future workshops can be found in critical social theory, more specifically in the theories of communication of Jürgen Habermas (1972). These methods were originally developed in the Federal Republic of Germany by Robert Jungk. In the 1950s Jungk joined a group of researchers who opposed the future-studies research derived from the American military think-tank concept, which was based on operations research. He was motivated by what he saw as a weakening of democracy, with politicians and planners no longer interested in public participation. Together with colleagues, Jungk opposed this tendency—whose goal was to increase human power over nature—by creating alternative methods of TA whose goal was to develop human and social predictions within the democratic process adopted by future workshops (Lund and Christensen 1986). Jungk worked closely with the Dutch philosopher Fred Polak (1971), who used historic examples to show how important the influence of future visions can be on the present. For example, visions influenced by resignation and anxiety can become self-fulfilling prophecies. Consider the case of nuclear energy: if it is believed to be the only solution to increasing demand, then alternative options are not sought.

If human visions and a democratization of the decision-making process are part of the goal of TA, future workshops become an obvious choice of method (Lund and Christensen 1986). Their major drawbacks are that they are time-consuming and can be expensive, and that it can be very difficult to select the appropriate representatives, bring them together, and motivate them.

Table 2
Frequently Used TA Methods

Method	Question Addressed
Cost-benefit analysis	Does the introduction of this technology pay off?
Cost-effectiveness analysis	Which is the most effective technology, using given resources?
Systems analysis	How and why does this system as a whole function as it does?
Risk assessment	What is the risk of introducing this technology, and is it worth taking?
Meta-analysis	What, according to the literature, is the average effect of this technology?
Controlled clinical trials	Does the technology have an effect that can be measured?
Delphi Technique	What do the experts predict the consequences of this technology to be?
Consensus conferences	What is the status of expert knowledge and the opinion of the interested parties with regard to this technology?
Public inquiries	What does the public have to say about this technology?
Social experiments	How can we develop social organization and learn ways to work with this technology?
Future workshops	How can democratic social action be generated in relation to this new technology?

Summary

This chapter has attempted to lay a foundation for an understanding of the phenomenon of TA by introducing and critiquing the methods of assessment most frequently used. Table 2 is an overview of these methods.

4
Problems Perceived by Proponents

There is general agreement that technology should be assessed, a positive attitude so common that Wynne (1975) called TA "a prime contender for the title of the latest good thing to arrive on the political scene." The question, then, is how it should be done. Although TA as such is not new, its having become a matter of public concern has placed it within the sphere of public influence and public funding. It is the organization of publicly funded TA that is recent, making it difficult to evaluate the long-term effects of TA or to foresee its long-term problems. Still, TA's proponents are aware of certain problems, both general and specific.

General Problems

One major issue is the fact that industry has not been enthusiastic about TA outside its domain. Emphasizing the danger that might inhibit innovation and progress, industries are reluctant to hire outside experts to do TA for them or to get involved unless they have to. A government official in Belgium recently related in an EC meeting on the subject that industry still regards TA as a hindrance to production and competition. He explained this attitude by what he perceived as the dominant economic philosophy: everything that can be produced should be produced; everything that is technologically feasible should be done; everything that can find a buyer should be offered for sale (Meyer 1991). As long as this is the prevalent attitude, industry will see TA as a hindrance, exactly as environmental legislation has been interpreted as a hindrance.

A very important consideration is the time factor: that is, when the assessment is done and what actions can be taken for avoiding potentially negative consequences. The question is whether it is not already too late for socially oriented systematic TA to influence the direction technology is taking. Christensen and Sigmund (1986) claim that TA is based on ideal demands which in general cannot be fulfilled. When there are no laws that require TA prior to marketing, it often happens that the TA results come after the technology has already been widely disseminated or when the technology in question has already been replaced by a newer one.

This was the case in Denmark in the late 1970s when the National Board of Health was asked to change the indications for using amniocentesis as a preventive measure against birth defects. At that time amniocentesis was offered to pregnant women who were over thirty-five years old or considered to be "at risk." When pressured to make the test available to all pregnant women, the National Board of Health initiated a series of randomized CCTs to assess the advantages and disadvantages of doing so. The study concluded that it was not advisable to make the test available to all women, because it appeared to increase the risk of abortion among normal, young pregnant women. But by the time this scientific evidence was made public in 1986, the technology was already being replaced by new technology, which—as was initially the case with amniocentesis—had not been subject to assessment.

Some critics question the "potency" of TA, the approach, and the potential effects. More specifically, a major weakness of TA pointed out by social scientists is that the approach sometimes referred to as "impact research" is most often retrospective (Koch and Morgall 1987).

The criticism was summed up by Winner (1986, 10) in the following way:

> An unfortunate shortcoming of technology assessment is that it tends to see technological change as a "cause" and everything that follows as an "effect" or "impact." The role of the researcher is to identify, observe, and explain these effects. This approach assumes that the causes have already occurred or are bound to do so in the normal course of events. Social research boldly enters the scene to study the "consequences" of the change. After the bulldozer has rolled over us, we pick ourselves up and carefully measure the treadmarks. Such is the impotent mission of technological "impact" assessment.

Still, although proactive assessment is the preferred choice of proponents, retrospective assessment should not be underestimated, as it can produce important knowledge and is preferable to pure effect analysis.

Another criticism derives from simple skepticism: can TA have any effect on technological development at all? Even though government regulation and intervention is expected, and in many cases has become a public demand, can governments on the one hand be relied on to prioritize the public interest over political and economic interests? On the other hand, can governments be expected to work together with industry to guide technological development as suggested by those who promote constructive technology assessment?

Constructive technology assessment requires a close relationship between state authorities and private industry. Its goal is to ensure an early impact of technology policy on technological innovations. Besides the disenchantment with state intervention expressed by many international agencies, there is criticism of too much public involvement in economic development. The problem for constructive TA is to determine appropriate and effective policy instruments to guide the innovations. This means offering attractive incentives and relevant ways to penalize undesired development. Examples can be found in the literature on environmental protection.

In discussing the effectiveness of TA, Tuininga (1988) points out problems in how governments deal with decisions about scientific and technical matters. These negative tendencies can be summarized as (1) a tendency for governments to define broad political problems in narrow technical terms, leading to closed politics which exclude the general public from decision-making; (2) a tendency to "parcel out" parts of issues for special treatment by each competent ministry, leading to a loss of overall perspective; (3) a tendency toward government dependence on technical expertise with a bias toward technical solutions, leading to the submersion of political choices in debates over optimistic technical feasibility.

A major problem for those people who want or are compelled to do TA is often the lack of an explicit technology policy in most Western societies.[1] As mentioned previously, very little proactive TA has been done outside industry. Since proactive TA depends on a general policy analysis approach, it presupposes well-thought-out societal needs.

Private industries have always had some sort of technology policy. They know what they want (profit, good products, positive public image, productive employees, and so on) and use technology to help them attain these goals. Governments, however, have a more difficult time defining the goals of society, especially in the West, where the power and wealth of the private sector often leave governments *unable* to plan without raising the specter of social and economic constrictions. Although a general surveillance of technological change seems to be universally accepted, policy analysis has had limited success, partly because of this lack of long-term planning by most governments.[2]

Inherent in the lack of long-term goals in the public sector is confusion about the aims of converting research results into practical politics. At the research level, this problem becomes one of deciding which variables should be studied in a government-funded or -supported assessment. There can be confusion among public administrations and politicians as to what is important and of public interest, as the following example demonstrates. In 1979 the Danish government asked its economic advisers to review the consequences of not building nuclear energy plants in Denmark.[3] Surprisingly enough, the Economic Council sent the request back, saying that in the members' opinion a real assessment could take place only if a wide variety of social aspects (not just economics) were also assessed (Müller, Remmen, and Christensen 1986).[4]

For people carrying out TA, there is also the problem of changing governments. Sudden shifts from left to right or the reverse (as has happened in southern Europe, as well as most recently in East European countries) can interrupt previously made, long-term social goals. Changes in government or government policy are followed by periods of inactivity while new priorities are being set.[5] A related problem is "impotent" governments attempting to function in incompatible and unstable coalitions under which a realistic technology policy is virtually impossible.[6]

Another political problem is deciding which technology should be assessed. The rapid advances in information technology, biotechnology, and alternative energy supplies (to name but a few) are all of potential concern to the present and future well-being of the general public. But since public funds could never finance assessments of each and every new technology, how should limited research funds be distributed? Which human needs should be met? Which social problems are the most pressing? What are the social priorities? What should the research priorities be?

There is an inherent conflict in government-funded TA. Whereas the government has a mandate to protect the nation's economic basis, it faces a conflict between the demands of a technology-based industry and the ever growing social costs of some technologies.

Despite all the foregoing criticisms, TA is generally regarded as positive. It is a tool available to the general public (perhaps the *only* tool) for exerting influence on the regulation and control of technological development. In a report published by the Danish Social Science Research Council, Cronberg (1986, 97) put it this way: "The majority of [TA] research projects fall within a paradigm, namely, one that assumes that technology can be controlled. We are now in a historic situation where the need for control of technological development is great but at the same time the *possibility is small*. We are optimistic and hope that our research can contribute to revealing control mechanisms and their limits."[7] It should be noted that practitioners of TA in Denmark are optimistic, and public debate is lively. The big problem facing Denmark and other small countries is that their fate with regard to technology and technological development is intimately tied to international politics and economics, especially the EC.

The Problem of Interested Parties

According to Salomon (1988), the entire history of industrialization can be seen as "the conflict between the consequences of technical change and the political effort to control these consequences." He identifies what he calls "four general political lessons" to be learned from this evolution: (1) that scientific and technical affairs can no longer be confined to scientific circles, as they have been by tradition; (2) that the legitimation of necessary decisions and society's support for technical change call for a decision-making process that is no longer solely in the hands of technicians, whether professional scientists or professional politicians; (3) that the nature, pace, and direction of technical change depend on regulatory mechanisms that should involve as many members of society as possible; (4) that there is a need to counter the monopolization of any particular technology. All four "lessons" support the demand made by social movements and pressure groups for a democratic TA. A democratic TA seeks to involve as many points of view as possible. The more social groups are involved, the more potential impacts may be recognized and more desirable options generated.

Although it is important to involve interested parties, *whose* interests should be taken into consideration, and how can different interests be reconciled? In realizing the goal of a democratic TA, many practical as well as methodological problems arise. I call these "the problems of interested parties," which I have divided into three issues: increasing mistrust of experts, public involvement and partisan research.

Increasing Mistrust of Experts
The public attitude toward experts has been changing from one of respect for authority to one of mistrust. This mistrust grows in step with public dependence on experts. Technology increasingly affects our everyday lives, at work as well as at home. This happens without our understanding technology and without technology's helping us to better understand ourselves. Households today produce less and less of their own food, clothing, and other necessities and so are more dependent on outside services. New workplace and household technology is more difficult to understand than the old mechanical versions and is therefore less likely to be repaired by its users. All this leads to a dependence on experts that gives

them power and influence in conflicts over technology. Although dependent on them, therefore, society and government often fear and mistrust experts.[8]

What are the interests and values of these "experts," the people and professions implicated in technical change? The TA debate has been dominated by scientists and civil servants (Dickson 1984). In his political lessons, Salomon (1988) emphasizes that scientific technical affairs can no longer be limited to scientific circles. Perhaps public mistrust can be explained by the simple fact that the experts, the policy-makers, and the public all have different agendas. As a concept, TA seeks to renew consideration of the role that science and technology play in today's society, thus providing an opportunity to redefine the role of experts.

The power of expert advice comes from the authority of scientific expertise, which rests on assumptions about scientific rationality. "Interpretations and predictions made by scientists are judged to be rational because they are based on data gathered through rational procedures. Their interpretations therefore serve as a basis for planning and as a means for defending the legitimacy of policy decisions" (Nelkin 1979, 15).

Should this "scientific rationality" be the basis for planning? The belief that it should is exactly what is being challenged by social movements, criticized by critical academics, and questioned by feminists. Today, such issues as nuclear power, leaded gasoline, pollution, biotechnology, contraception safety, drug safety, and workplace safety have become more political than technical. Non-institutionalized TA groups, more than any others, have recognized that technical expertise is a crucial *political* resource. The government's role is to establish and arbitrate a balance between groups with conflicting interests in TA. Yet a case may often be resolved on the basis of "the relative strengths of interested parties" (Noble 1979, 19) rather than on justice, an outcome that "influences the status of scientific and technical knowledge. Different interest groups frequently attempt to use experts and scientific information to back up their case, thus undermining the status of such knowledge claims generally" (Mumford 1983, 245).

Once the perception of science and technology has been altered and expertise has become a resource, then

> whether or not the knowledge or expertise is "correct" in any absolute sense becomes secondary to the status of knowledge as "knowledge," which in turn depends on such matters as the status of the expert and the source of the information. Knowledge has become very closely related to power: when all the experts back up a government department, local authority or firm with their scientific information, then those bodies appear to be all-powerful. When some people disagree, and back their argument with expert knowledge that challenges what has previously been accepted as "the facts," then that power is also challenged. Thus, decision-making in areas which had previously been seen as part of a paradigm of shared rationality and consensus, has begun to take on an adversarial, or negotiated character. [Coombs, Saviotti, and Walsh 1987, 217]

This polarization weakens the credibility of scientific knowledge among the public. Scientific knowledge is no longer seen as objective, pure, esoteric, and inaccessible to the public; hence it is devalued in the public's opinion and experts mistrusted.

Non-institutionalized sources of TA claim that our understanding of technical change, where appropriate, must take new sources of information into account. The consequences of institutionalized TA as well as the influence of firms, markets, and government policies shape the process of technical change in a complex way. This is particularly the case of large-scale and visible technical choices. The outcomes often contribute to changes in the boundaries between firms, markets, and state agencies and their relative influence over the technology in question (Coombs, Saviotti, and Walsh 1987).

Of course, the fields of science and technology have knowledge interests at various levels. For example, in the context of the labor market, salary, job description, professional status, and the like can give employers or employees a vested interest that may be in conflict with public interests.[9] The general public may well fear that those experts who have no social conscience will be willing to work for anyone who is willing to pay (Teknologistyrelsen 1984).[10]

The power of definition that professionals perpetuate with their "expert knowledge" is obvious in the following example from my own study of prescription drug use from a users' perspective (Hansen, Launsoe, and Morgall 1989). Pharmacists have been taught that noncompliance—that is, the widespread and common practice of not following the prescribed instructions for the use of drugs—is deviant behavior on the part of the patient. The results of this study found that noncompliance was more often a conscious decision on the users' part, not neglect or a misunderstanding of the instructions. It was a form of "self-regulation." In interviewing prescription drug users, I found that this misinterpretation of the causes of noncompliance could be traced to health care personnel's practice of transferring expert knowledge to users without taking into consideration the patients' own experience with medications (sometimes spanning a lifetime), or the effects of the drugs on the social context of the users' daily lives. This lack of regard for their own experience was at the root of the anxiety and mistrust that users expressed about the experts.

In summing up this critique of experts, I should mention that the literature on empowerment deals directly with the question of expertise and rests on a radical critique of the professions. In brief, it points out that, too often, professionals have misappropriated their specialized knowledge to serve their own interests, as well as those of a power elite intent on maintaining its own dominance over the rest of society (Fischer 1990).

Public Involvement
In trying to live up to the public pressure for democratic TA, policy-makers have attempted to involve the public. This has created both political and methodological problems: how to select public representatives, and how to involve them in the TA process. Nelkin (1977) points out that problems in achieving public participation include deciding who should be involved, who represents the interests of the public, what constitutes a legitimate interest, and who represents that interest. Political conflicts, she emphasizes, cannot be ignored.

The increase in the number of pressure groups and the impact of social movements on TA result from the fact that a group is more effective than an individual. An effective course of action for the ordinary citizen who wants to influence decisions about technology is to get someone of recognized authority to act on his or her behalf: trade unions, or politicians, or other people with similar interests or views.[11] Involving the public either as individuals or as groups can be both time-consuming and expensive for policy-makers. It can also be a problem to identify individuals who represent the "general" public. Wilkinson (1983, 22) has suggested the following approach. First, it is important to identify the interests and values of those actors or interest groups who are implicated in the technical change (engineers, managers, groups of workers, and so on). Then one must ask, how do they perceive the change and what do they expect to gain or lose from it? At what stage of technical change do interest groups and coalitions attempt to impose their own aims (design, trial, implementation)?

Another central problem, for the groups attempting to influence science and technology policy as well as for the government agencies initiating participatory experiments, is how to create an informed citizenry (Nelkin, 1979). For example, it has been difficult to find "qualified" participants for consensus conferences: that is, people who are able to follow the technical aspects of the discussion and who possess the ability to argue for the desires and needs of society in general. A common phenomenon is what I call the "professional consumer," a person with consumer experience who is repeatedly asked to represent the public on a variety of issues.[12] Plans to involve societal groups in the TA process can be found in the still rather vague "social address" concept. This is intended as a means of collecting signals that could lead to the formulation of questions and ideas for national TA programs. It is also seen as a method of involving groups that otherwise would be absent from research programs (Smits and Leyten 1988).

Partisan Technology Assessment
It is necessary to distinguish between the efforts of interested parties and what I refer to as "partisan research" and "partisan assessment."[13] The term "interest groups" denotes people with a stake in the development of technology, whether at a very early stage (research and development); during the diffusion phase (marketing and promotion); as the end user, recipient, or group implicated at the implementation phase; or as a special interest group not necessarily affected by this technology but having a broader interest in the issues at large.[14] "Partisan assessment" refers to the activities of various "parties" or "partners" who will be involved and have an interest in the actual assessment. They may not even have an *interest* per se in the assessment other than as hired hands: that is, researchers. Partisan research is a specific aspect of acknowledging and involving interested groups in TA. It also occurs when an interest group initiates its own TA. For example, in Scandinavia during the 1970s it was com-

mon for unions to hire academics to study the effects of
new technology on workplace environment or to investigate occupational health hazards.

The following example of how various interest groups
view partisan research illustrates the conflicting interests
and different opinions about what constitutes a "democratic" TA, as well as industry's opposition. As a result of
the first report (Teknologiraadet 1980) by the Technology
Committee under the Technology Council (Ministry of Industry) in Denmark, a rather heated debate arose around
the issue of "partisan research." The report concluded
that technology development and TA could no longer be
left solely to industry and to the technicians, economists,
and jurists employed within public administration. The
reason given was that these people would make narrow
assessments based on the usual considerations growing
from their own education and work experience.[15] The
committee therefore suggested the establishment of three
subcommittees to decide annually how the TA budget
should be divided among four areas: (1) projects of an
overall, long-term nature within areas that the committee
found necessary; (2) projects connected to professional organizations and grassroots movements; (3) partisan projects connected to working life from an employees' perspective; (4) partisan projects connected to working life
from a management perspective.[16]

The Technology Council considered this proposal an
attack on the legal right of management in the private
sector to "organize and delegate work." It labeled partisan research "prostitution," in that the research would
give up its "independent" approach.[17] The Technology
Council forwarded the report to the Ministry of Industry
with the comment that it did not agree with the practice
of partisan research, or with the idea that TA should be
removed from the auspices of the Ministry of Industry to
the Technology Committee, as suggested. In 1984 the second report of the Technology Council came out—with one

major omission. There was not a word about "partisan" research. Strangely enough, the 1984 report did include reference to action research as well as a holistic TA that would include all interested parties, but this reference was not elaborated upon (Christensen and Sigmund 1986).

The protest made by industry through the Technology Council is a good illustration of the belief that as soon as "outsiders" get mixed up with the assessment and the decision-making process, the character of TA changes from objective research to political instrument. It is yet another example of the hostile attitude that industry has developed for TA done outside its domain and illustrates the opposition that partisan TA faces. Although partisan TA is an essential issue in TA, it has not been an issue for public debate in countries other than Denmark, perhaps because it is usually masked by such issues as dealing with special interests, involving the public, and defining long-term social policy.

There are many problems facing non-institutionalized TA. One is the lack of funds, another the limited access to information. And finally, small pressure groups (including feminists) often lack power and credibility, especially if they go against the popular perception of technology as social progress and suggest alternatives to technological innovations.

Methodological Problems

If the political problems associated with TA are basically questions of *who*, then methodological problems are a question of *how*. Methodological problems are concerned with the inclusion and exclusion criteria of variables: how to assess and how to involve implicated parties. How will conflicting interests be taken into consideration? How should we evaluate qualitative consequences? How does one assess noncomparable aspects in relation to one another? How do we determine what weight should be given to different aspects?[18]

In any assessment, there are normative considerations: that is, implicit and unclear measurements for and acceptance of the social and human values that are used as the basis for assessment. Very often, these are not consciously known, even by those who use them. Joergensen (1986) thinks it important to make these measurements for assessment explicit so that they can be objects of conscious reflection. For research purposes, this means that criteria based on human, social, and cultural values that could form the measurement for TA must be made scientific. Problems of definition and of inclusion and exclusion criteria frequently arise, especially in multidisciplinary research groups, where each discipline has its own paradigm and its own traditional and preferred methods (Launsoe and Rieper 1987).

Difficulties with definitions in TA can be seen as partially political and partially methodological.[19] If there is no overall technology policy, on what social criteria should the measurements be based? On what theory of technology and society should the research be based? How should one decide what technology needs to be assessed?

Remmen (1986) ascribes methodological difficulties to the fact that there are often no distinctions made between method and procedure. For example, there may be confusion between methods of measurement and questions of how to establish and work in a multidisciplinary research team or how to make useful contacts with the technical sources. One problem is that commonly used methods have their origins in a variety of research disciplines: future studies, economic analysis, evaluation studies, working-life research, and others. TA becomes what Christensen and Sigmund (1986) call a "dust bin" of methodology served up under a new label.

What I consider the major problem of TA is the fact

that knowledge and organizational interests play an important role in the development of technology yet are seldom taken into consideration at the assessment stage (Koch and Morgall 1987; Morgall and Vedel 1985; Noble 1979; Remmen 1986). Hoos (1982, 2) is an outspoken critic of methods used in TA, specifically cost-benefit analysis and the systems analysis approach. She claims that a critical assessment must question the purpose and the methods used, as well as the assumptions supported. It must make known the fact that TA is not a neutral, objective exercise free of value commitments or wider social context. She further advises that it is important to know not only the purpose of the assessment but who pays for the research, since funds are often expended "to serve vested and not the public interest."

Methodological problems arise because TA lacks an agreed-upon theoretical basis. The literature is dominated first by empirical studies and second by methodological discussions, both of which, more often than not, lack theoretical bases. This is often the case in policy-oriented TA, less frequently in research-oriented TA. When theory *is* explicitly presented, it is usually in those assessments initiated by the social and human sciences.[20]

Methodological problems are exacerbated by a lack of theoretical underpinnings, as manifested in methods that are nothing more than techniques and are therefore atheoretical; methods that are implicitly linked to theory even though reference is never made to that theory; methods that ignore the impact of technology on specific groups because the implicit theories are not equipped to deal with issues of power, socioeconomic differences, or gender.

Summary
This chapter distinguishes between various approaches and knowledge interests as they affect TA and MTA methods. Among the many problems facing a democratic

development of assessment is the involvement of interested parties in the assessment process, which I consider a prerequisite for a gender analysis.

Other major problems are the opposition of industry, which is not only unenthusiastic about public TA but at times even hostile; the skepticism even of proponents who wonder whether TA can have any effect or whether we are too late; doubts as to the potency of whatever effect TA does have.

Political problems include governments' lack of long-term societal goals, lack of or unclear technology policy, confusion about aims, dealing with changing governments, and prioritizing the technologies to be assessed.

Then there are the problems of interested parties: confronting the increasing public mistrust of experts, identifying conflicting interests, ensuring and determining the extent of the involvement of interested parties, and incorporating partisan research in assessment projects.

Methodological problems include how to develop inclusion and exclusion criteria; how to clarify implicit measurements for and improve acceptance of the social and human values used as the basis of assessment; how to measure and assess non-comparable aspects in relation to each other, a question in part related to the major methodological problem—the neglect of theory.

It can be concluded that TA has neither a common theory nor agreed-upon methods, and that their absence causes problems of validity. This is especially true when the goal is a comprehensive TA that will analyze the consequences of technology in the context of everyday life. Such an analysis must deal with the reality of dominance, control, and conflicting values, which is the essence of gender analysis.

PART II
Women
and
Technology

5

A Feminist Perspective
on Technology

I see the various approaches and methods used in TA as representing different perceptions of technological development. Whether these perceptions are based on well-thought-out theories or are expressed simply as a viewpoint or an impression, each one reflects an interpretation of the role of technology in society. The interpretation can be either an implicit, an explicit, or a totally unconscious choice. This chapter, by presenting the feminist scholarship on technological development, identifies areas of feminist studies that can contribute to a more comprehensive and critical TA.

How a Feminist Perspective Evolved
Before about 1970, "women and technology" was a non-topic. Today there are numerous journals and books and hundreds of articles on the subject. General interest evolved in the 1970s when the women's movement began questioning why so few women were entering the fields of science, technology, and medicine. This discussion moved from asking why more women don't even try to pondering why women do it at all.

The inquiry into the recruitment of women and minorities paralleled a critical analysis of the limitations of the natural and social sciences. In the 1960s and 1970s critical scientists and social scientists sought to explain the origin and growth of modern science and technology in terms of the needs of a burgeoning capitalist society. This social constructionist view of science found dominant social relations to be constitutive of science.[1] Together with other social movements, the women's movement drew inspiration from the critique of mainstream science and technology, which until that time had been formulated as sex-neutral (Bermann 1988). That view eventually changed, first to approaches that focused on the social relations helping to shape technology and then, through the work of feminist scholars, to an approach that moved a step further and included the effects of gender: "Technological processes have been studied from the (usually implicit) vantage point of men's experience. When one puts women at the center of analysis, male biases and masculinized ideologies become clearer, and one discovers new questions as well as fresh approaches to old questions" (Kramarae 1988, 7).

Another source of inspiration was the labor process debate in the 1970s and 1980s.[2] Many feminist authors who have studied women and technology (I include myself) have been influenced by the labor process debate, as well as by the social constructionist analysis of science and technology.[3] But though feminist scholars were inspired by both bodies of research, they criticized the labor studies not only because they were gender blind but because they evinced another major weakness: they focused exclusively on production.[4] Feminist scholars pointed out that this is a typical way in which gender as a variable can "legitimately" be ignored. In contrast, feminist studies have focused on the tension and conflict between the productive and reproductive spheres as an essential element in understanding women's role in society.

Relatively few academically oriented feminists were interested in technology before the 1980s, when they began to theorize the relationship of man and machine and trace its history (Arnold and Faulkner 1985; Rothschild 1983; Zimmermann 1983). A characteristic of the women's movement in the late 1980s, and a feature missing from earlier phases, was the demand for women to have access to technological knowledge, skills, and jobs (Cockburn 1989). These efforts resulted in the setting up of practical training initiatives for women in the United Kingdom, the United States, and parts of Europe, including Scandinavia.

What a Feminist Perspective Is
It was feminists and historians who drew out the gender-specific nature of the view of technology as progress (Rose 1987). Feminists criticized what they saw as male-dominated development, especially the long-standing tradition of modern Western science as a masculine endeavor. In studies in the fields of science and technology, feminist scholars have specifically addressed problems and issues such as male dominance, the active exclusion of women, lack of interest in the role of technology in everyday life, the role of the state in technological development, and differing values between men and women with regard to technology.

Male dominance in the development and control of technology was one of the initial themes explored. Feminist studies brought attention to the fact that men design, finance, buy, sell, and set technology in motion (Morgall 1983a). Male dominance can be found within all stages of technological development: the laboratory stage (research and development), the introductory stage (industrial sector), the dissemination stage (marketing and advertising), and even the assessment stage (public and private sectors as well as academia). At each stage the social meaning of technology is being constructed and reconstructed. The underrepresentation of women in technological development is seen as a reflection of asymmetric power relations between the sexes in society in general.

The exclusion of women from the fields of science and technology is another theme.[5] That active forces were at work to keep women out has been documented. In his most recent work the historian David Noble (1992b) traces the roots of a masculine science and technology over the last thousand years, back to the practices and institutions of higher learning that were dominated by male Christian clerics: "The male monopoly on science is no mere relic to be easily tossed aside. Throughout most of its evolution, science has not simply excluded women; it has been defined in defiance of women and in their absence. The field has remained an alien world for them, one where they face not just discrimination but dread" (1992a, 54). In 1662, for example, the Royal Society was established in Britain as the first official organization of natural philosophers. Its announced aim was to "raise a Masculine philosophy . . . whereby the Mind of Man may be ennobled with the knowledge of solid truths" (quoted in Easlea 1981). A further example is that until the early 1900s it was common practice to exclude women from medical schools in Western cultures (Ehrenreich and English 1979).

Cockburn (1985b, 1986) shows how male dominance has largely been secured by the active exclusion of women from areas of technologically based work: for example, the printing industry. She goes so far as to say that technology is "both the social property and one of the formative processes of men." A further elaboration of this theme addresses what is known in feminist research as "the invisible woman" phenomenon: that is, the practice of ignoring women's participation and achievements in recorded history. Hynes (1989a) calls it the "razing of women's technical achievements." Early efforts made by feminist academics to trace the history of women and their innovations include the works of Trescott (1979) and Warner (1979). Later efforts were made not only to explore the participation but to make visible the role, contribution, and specific professional accomplishments of women through concrete examples. The work of Fox Keller (1985) and Stanley (1981) are examples of this scholarship.

Social class has been shown to have played an important part in women's role in science and technology. This was especially true when science was considered a craft; at that time the daughters and wives of scientists enjoyed a certain privileged access to laboratories (Rose 1986). Modern-day versions echo this theme of privileged class origins and the unusual support and encouragement of either a father or a husband (Fox Keller 1985; Rose 1986; Walden 1982).

Ignoring women or making them invisible is the basis of the critique feminists level against mainstream academia. But this exclusion is not limited to women as such; it is rather a reflection of an academic unconcern with technology in everyday life. The tendency to prioritize high-powered technology can be found in the studies done on the modern history of technology. In a content analysis of twenty-four years of the American publication *Technology and Culture*, founded in 1958, Rothschild (1983) found only four articles on women-related subjects—the first not until 1976—and only one of them dealt with a topic other than technology in housework. Otherwise, the study of technology had been defined and treated as a historical discipline and focused on the man-machine relationship. Nor can one find discussions of any child-care devices in the standard histories of technology written by men. For example, there is not a single reference to one simple implement that had a significant impact on society: the baby bottle (Cowan 1979).

Another feminist interest has been the role of the state

in technological development. The state is seen as having an important role to play at every stage of technological development.[6] In this context, feminist authors have criticized the state for its control of the legal framework in which the development and use of technology are embedded (Kirejczyk 1988).[7] "The logic of a state that is both capitalist and patriarchal requires that there is continuous change but that the fundamental structures of power are left undisturbed. For the state, managing science and technology is always crisis management, as new knowledge and new technologies always offer—or seem to offer—the possibility of social change" (Rose 1987, 169). The state has indirect power to license the use of various technologies (or the potential to do so in the future). The state also has the responsibility and the power to control the dissemination of technology, which has implications for TA.

Whether occurring under the supervision of the state or in a private institution, education and training and women's experiences with them have also been important areas of study. Cockburn (1989) and Berner (1985) point out the important role that education and training have played in perpetuating sex typing in technical occupations—even to the point of excluding women from technical and scientific studies, a phenomenon explained in historical detail by Noble (1992b). Rose (1986) makes the interesting point that not only has it been difficult for women to get into science and technology; it has also been very difficult for them to stay in.

The issues addressed by feminists have resulted in the development of four major fields of inquiry: (1) the impact of female-male dualism in science and technology (Easlea 1983; Fox Keller 1985; Griffin 1978; Gray 1979; Merchant 1980; Noble 1992b); (2) the effect of technology on women's roles in production (Huws 1982; Vedel 1982); and reproduction (Corea 1985, 1989; Firestone 1970; Koch

1986; Russ 1975); (3) women as active contributors and inventors of technology and their influence and invisibility in technological development (Alic 1981; Bergom-Larsson 1982; Stanley 1981; Trescott 1979); (4) the experience of women technicians during training for and work in male-dominated technology fields (Berner 1982, 1984; Bruvik-Hansen, Billing, and Rasmussen 1983; Kolmos 1989; Kvande 1982; Rossiter 1979).

These fields of inquiry have at least two things in common. First, they regard technology as a form of human, social, and cultural activity and therefore totally reject the perception of it as a neutral tool (technological determinism); second, they all attempt to explain, in one way or another, the role of technology not only as it performs certain tasks but also as it creates personal or competitive advantages for some and not for others.

In general, feminist scholars research technology as it relates to human activities and situations, viewing it as either advantageous or disadvantageous for women. Bush (1983) represents this approach, which regards technology as an equity issue. Inequalities resulting from technological changes as they occur in the labor and health care sectors have been a constant theme (Ehrenreich and English 1979; Feminist Review 1986; Ratcliff 1989; Whitelegg et al. 1982). Feminist studies have been less interested in inventions than in the use and users of technology, including the subsequent effects on the environment and cultural conditions (among them, sex/gender roles). They tend to analyze technology in its social context and to emphasize the importance of social factors—such as women's work, lives, and status—in shaping technological change.

The feminist studies have not evolved from just one academic discipline; interdisciplinary studies have been characteristic throughout. These studies can in fact be considered a process of redefinition and integration of existing disciplines. Therefore, studies of women and technology can be found in history, psychology, cultural geography, sociology, and economics.

Theoretical Grounding

It has been characteristic of feminist studies that there is no one single theory or perspective. Thus it follows that no one accepted theory or method exists for a feminist approach to technological development.

There are, however, three areas in the study of technology where feminist scholarship has distinguished itself.

1 *Analyzing science and technology as part of a system of domination.* This was done by introducing the theory of patriarchy and theories of capitalism into an analysis of interests and power.

2 *Further developing the division-of-labor analysis.* Central to the women's technology analysis is the division of labor and the role that technology plays in maintaining control over women's labor and women's lives.

3 *Making an analysis of values an important part of technology research.* Different and often opposing value systems develop with the introduction of technological innovations.

I discuss these areas of study here, separately and as they relate to each other. I argue that each of them can contribute to the further development of TA (see Chapter 6).

Systems of Domination

The feminist approach to technological development has distinguished itself by focusing on issues of domination, power, and control.[8] This was done primarily by introducing theories of patriarchy. Patriarchy as a concept is used to describe the dominance of men over women, which manifests itself in various ways in society. According to theories of patriarchy, the introduction of technology becomes a tool for maintaining the oppression of women in society, on the labor market, and at home.

Several approaches to defining and theorizing patriarchy have developed.[9] Some theories explain women's oppression as a psychological, ideological, or cultural phenomenon. These theories can be criticized as either ahistoric or too psychological for the purposes of the sociological study of technology.[10] Approaches to patriarchy have also evolved within the social sciences. One such approach, growing out of critical social theory, developed a material base for sex/gender differences. This branch of women's studies has made a considerable contribution to studies of women and technology, especially of technology in the labor market. I found this approach important in analyzing technological development in the clerical and health care sectors.

In the Marxist-feminist tradition, patriarchy is defined as a set of social relations which has a material base, and where hierarchical relations between and solidarity among men enable them to control women (Hartmann 1981). The basic concepts found in critical women's studies are women's experience with capitalism and patriarchy. There has been disagreement between two theoretical perspectives, each explaining the relation between class and sex/gender in its own way: dual system theory, positing that capitalism and patriarchy are two separate systems in continual interaction with each other; and single system theory, arguing that they are parts of the same social system, which combines both mode of production and sex/gender hierarchies.[11]

Dual system theory emerged in an attempt to reconcile Marxist social theory and feminist theory. There are several versions, though all agree that "patriarchal relations designate a system of relations distinct from and in-

dependent of the relations of production described by traditional Marxism" (Young 1981).[12]

I believe that single system theory best describes the
development of science and technology as part of a system of domination, because it recognizes the class oppression that affects all workers in this development. It also
recognizes that a hierarchical, sex-differentiated power
structure exists. As Young (1981, 61) argues:

> One can . . . explain the sexism of male workers without
> appealing to a system of social relations independent of
> capitalism, by seeing the essentially patriarchal character
> of the system of capitalism itself. One explains it by seeing
> how capitalism is an economic system in which a gender
> division of labor having a historically specific form and
> structure . . . by marginalizing women's labor gives men a
> specific kind of privilege and status.

The single system theory recognizes that class functions are the core concept of the Marxist theory of social
relations. Since Marxist theory lacks an analysis of gender differentiation and gender hierarchy, advocates of the
single system theory propose remaining "within the mate-
rialist framework by elevating the category of division of
labor to a position as fundamental as, if not more fundamental than, that of class. This category can provide
us with the means of analyzing the social relations of la-
boring activity in a gender-differentiated way" (Young
1981, 51).

That the division of labor is more basic than class divisions in the capitalist system should be understood to
mean that the current class society in fact emerged
through a change in the sexual division of labor in precapitalist society; that is, the capitalist system developed
at a certain stage of male domination. Women's oppression under capitalism is not a coincidence. The sexual hierarchy in precapitalist society is the very basis upon
which class society later developed.

The single system theory argues that capitalism is

structured along gender lines which are a function of the structure and dynamics of capitalism itself. It sees the marginalization of women and their function as a secondary labor force as essential and fundamental characteristics of capitalism. It argues that the gender division of labor should always be a part—but never the only part—of the explanation of women's situation.

Within the framework of women's studies, both the dual and single system theories have been criticized by radical feminists for being overly economic, ignoring the psychological dimensions of patriarchy, accepting heterosexuality as an institution, and lacking a racial dimension. Critical theorists in nonfeminist literature have explored concepts of control and dominance in relation to technological development, examined the domination-of-nature theme, and found capitalist relations built into technology. Feminists have used patriarchy as the theoretical tool for providing an understanding of the control and dominance aspects of technological development for women.

I see Western science and technology as developing within a market economy that encourages a hierarchical system of domination, expressed in a complex division of labor and a division between work and home. This brings us to the sexual division of labor.

Division of Labor
A major feminist contribution to studies of technology has been the further development of the division-of-labor analysis.[13] The division of labor is central to women's technology analysis and to the role technology plays in maintaining control over women's labor and women's lives. The detailed and hierarchical division of labor by sex has been a fruitful area of study among feminist scholars over the years; from it developed studies of the implications of new technology as they affected the division of labor by sex.

The division of labor by sex manifests itself in many ways; that is, women's participation in the labor market has been significantly different from that of men. Historically, the ability of women to earn a living has depended on labor market demands (Huws 1982; Vedel 1982). Periods of economic growth (the Industrial Revolution or the early 1960s) or of acute labor shortages (wartime) led to a prioritization of public services that freed women from many domestic chores by establishing day care, modern housing, medical care. During periods of economic regression or religious/ideological repression, however, women (particularly single heads of households) have found it difficult if not impossible to live an economically independent life.

Moreover, women do not work in the same jobs as men. When during the 1970s feminist scholars began looking at the distribution of women on the job market, they found that one-third of all working women in the United States were concentrated in only seven job categories: clerical, domestic, retail sales, waitressing, bookkeeping, nursing, and teaching (Baxandall, Ewen, and Gordon 1976). In Sweden, women worked in only twenty-five of a total of 290 job categories; in fact, 75 percent of the women in Sweden were concentrated in only eighteen jobs (Goransson 1978). In Denmark, 70 percent of working women were concentrated in ten categories, and clerical jobs accounted for 20 percent of all working women (Borchorst 1984). This kind of job segregation is known as the *horizontal* division of labor by sex.

Besides not having the same jobs, women do not have the same job *status* as men. This is the *vertical* division of labor by sex. Although the division of labor by sex appears to have been universal throughout human history, in our society it is hierarchical, with men at the top and women at the bottom (Hartmann 1979).[14] There are fewer women than men in management and supervisory positions: 3 percent of women versus 14 percent of men in

Denmark (Ligestillingsraadet 1987).[15] The same is true for academia, especially in the fields of science and technology. Lauritzen (1990) studied women's status at two Danish universities during the late 1980s. She found not only a horizontal division of labor (very few women in the natural and technology sciences) but also an absence of women in any position of status or authority.

The vertical division of labor as it relates to technological development is examined in a study of recent forms of work organization as they relate to gender. Burris (1989) reports structural changes characterized by a polarization into "expert" and "non-expert" sectors. The reorganization of work is seen as paralleling and reinforcing sex segregation, with women disproportionately found in the non-expert category.

There has always been a *geographic* division of labor resulting from regional as well as urban-rural differences in job opportunities, and this affects women primarily (Vedel 1986). Today, however, what is called remote-based work is flourishing through the advances of information technology.

The sexual division of labor also has a *temporal* dimension characterized by part-time versus full-time work. In Scandinavia in the 1980s approximately 50 percent of all working women worked part time. In fact, the increase in the frequency of married women in the labor market was due to the increase in part-time work (Ipsen 1985). This led to a view of full-time work as men's work and part-time work as women's: nine-tenths of all part-time jobs in Denmark were held by women (Vedel 1986), the majority were in the clerical sector.

A major theme of feminist studies has been the significance of domestic labor—that is, mostly unpaid work—a major omission in many previous studies. During the rise of capitalism, old institutions were pulled down and new ones created, among them a free and open labor market that established low salaries for women. Consequently, it became possible to maintain women's dependence on men, at the same time that married women did housework for their husbands. Men received the advantages of both higher pay and the favorable division of labor at home (Hartmann 1981).

Women's housework and caring for others privately in the home represents a large portion of total work time in most countries today. Housework is characterized by long hours, a high rate of accidents, and social isolation. This kind of work is usually unpaid and invisible; that is, it is not measured or included in official labor statistics. Even though women have increasingly participated in the paid labor market (especially since World War II), they still have the major responsibility for housework and child care. This is what is referred to in the feminist literature as the "double day" or double work load.

The domestic sphere has also undergone technological development. Washing machines, electric irons, vacuum cleaners, dishwashers, and other devices were put into mass production and became available in the 1940s and 1950s. The claim that these machines would be time savers was true only to a point. Feminist scholars who analyzed the effect of household technology on women's domestic work found that it developed in direct relation to women's increased participation in the labor market (Cronberg 1986). In other words, the time saved was appropriated by the labor market and not as leisure time for women.

Studies worldwide show that since 1930 there has been little or no decrease in the amount of time a woman spends on unpaid labor, usually in the home (D'Onofrio-Flores and Pfafflin 1982). The nature of the work, however, has changed: whereas previously housework was physically taxing, it has shifted to time-consuming "personal services" performed for the family, such as shopping, general household management, and higher demands on child care.

In summary, the division of labor by sex takes several forms: horizontal, vertical, geographic, and temporal. These developments must all be seen within the context of women's double work load (their responsibility for domestic labor), which is the main limitation on both frequency and time of women's participation in the job market.

Values

The analysis of values is often considered the most important contribution made by feminists to studies in the field of technological development and assessment, but it is certainly also the most problematic. The problems are those of definition as well as analysis. Feminist literature, as a consequence of its multidisciplinary nature, uses the term "values" rather loosely. I use it to denote ideas held by groups about what they judge to be desirable, proper, good or bad—a form of visionary theorizing.

In philosophy, values are analyzed in the context of ethics, political philosophy, aesthetics, and epistemology. In the humanities, values are analyzed within the theoretical framework of cultures and subcultures. In the social sciences, values are studied as constituent facts of social structure, objects of socially conditioned desire, unevenly distributed and differentially ranked. In this presentation of the feminist analysis of values, I focus on the origins and consequences of the so-called masculine values that are said to be built into technology.

Within the field of sociology, the knowledge interests of science and technology have been an area of intense study. The Frankfurt school attempted to show how the metaphor and practice of domination ran as a central thread through the development of science (Rose 1986). Until the 1960s the male was the prototype used by most scholars in the study of technology: the male inventor and user of, thinker about, and reactor to technology. It was not until feminists included gender in this analysis of domination that science and technology became identified with masculine values.

A few exceptions among male scholars, however, broke through male prototypes, among them Lewis Mumford (1966, 1970). In the context of the technology-culture debates of the 1960s and 1970s, he argued that it is mental capacities that distinguish humans from other animal species, not the toolmaking capacity. He identified female qualities of visualization and imagination as present in the earliest techniques, which were meant to enhance human expression and to aid human beings in the task of recreating themselves. These early techniques were for use in everyday life and were neither work- nor power-related. With what he called the development of "megamachines" and the coming of "megatechnics" in our culture, however, this subjective (feminine) element became almost totally submerged. Mumford concluded that so-called female qualities had played an important role in technological development. He found subjective impulses and fantasies to have been formative influences in creating and transforming culture (Rothschild 1983).

Although Mumford's work has been criticized by feminists for its male linguistic conventions, there is widespread agreement with his discussion of the rational and objective characteristics of our science and technology.[16] He emphasized the importance of the role that the subjective, intuitive, and irrational can and do play in science and technology, a theme later taken up by several feminist authors (Fox Keller 1985; Hacker 1989; Trescott 1979).

The gender implications of science and technology can be found in the work of other male academics as well.[17] Since the 1960s, in fact, men have included gender in their attempts to explain current technological trends in war and the destruction of nature. Most comprehensive is the work of Brian Easlea (1980, 1981, 1983), whose research for a series of historic works on science and technology led him to investigate the relationship of these developments to sexual oppression. His study of the link between witch-hunting and the rise of science in the sixteenth and seventeenth centuries began with a Marxist materialistic analysis; however, he became convinced that noneconomic factors such as gender identity and sexual attitudes were needed to explain the ferocity of the persecutions, as well as their underlying causes. In 1983 Easlea extended this work to show, in a detailed study, how the seventeenth-century scientific revolution already contained the seeds of today's oppressive technologies. He traced the myths and metaphors associated with the "conquest of nature" through history to the role of the scientist today in nuclear arms production, uncovering what he labeled masculine values in the production of scientific knowledge. He concluded that the history of science and technology under capitalism is a history of men and domination. He called for a reevaluation of masculine institutions and ideologies. Easlea's work has contributed to feminist studies, even though he has been criticized for ignoring work done by women in this field (which, although limited, did exist at the time of his writing).

Feminist scholars have studied "controlling imagery" by analyzing gender. Values as they relate to the development of science and technology have been explored in a historical context by feminists.[18] For example, feminist theologians have demonstrated that the ideological roots of male dominance and masculine values can be found in Judeo-Christian cosmology. They claim that the imagery in the Bible's story of creation set gender roles that have remained largely unchanged.[19] Although Western science did not develop in competition with religion, it did eventually undermine the contemporary religious interpretation of reality (Eyerman 1985). It may not be too much to say that as one consequence, science as a system of beliefs slowly came to replace Christianity as the focal point of European civilization.

Male dominance in science and technology can be traced back to the origins of what feminists call the patriarchal nature of Western science. This is attributed to major developments in seventeenth-century Western Europe, when science and technology are said to have become identified with power, activism, and aggression (Nandy 1979) and these male values became embedded in new technology.

> One of the major problems with Western science and technology is that it has the historically determined male values built into it. These are the values of the White Male Warrior, admired for his strength and speed in eliminating the weak, conquering competitors and ruling over vast armies of men who obey his every instruction. He makes decisions which are logical and rational and which will lead to victory. [Cooley 1980, 43]

Caroline Merchant (1980) has produced what is considered the most thorough feminist development of the domination-of-nature theme. Focusing on what she calls the "ideologic shift"—the transition from an organic to a mechanistic world view—in science during the seventeenth century and singling out Francis Bacon as one of the most influential thinkers of the time, she draws attention to repeated metaphors of male domination, rape, and despoliation. Bacon referred to nature as a (female) slave, a whore who must be dominated, penetrated, and ruled. Merchant acknowledges that Bacon was not the originator of this controlling imagery; her further analysis uncovered the same recurring metaphor in the writings of scientists and philosophers of science since Greek and Roman times. Nevertheless, it is in the seventeenth-century ideologic shift that Merchant sees the transformation of social values which sanctioned the exploitation of the earth. An important attribute of the mechanistic paradigm is the belief that nature consists of two separate and independent realms: mind and matter. Although the transformation of values was neither abrupt nor absolute, Merchant finds the masculinist theory and practice of the domination of nature at the root of the paradigm of science and technology we have today. She identifies several reasons why the one intellectual paradigm (mechanistic) surpassed the other (organic): material factors provided a hospitable climate;[20] "progress" required a rational social order; the power to manage and control society, nature, and resources became available; the Protestant Reformation and the rise of commercial capitalism and science added their influence.

Merchant has been criticized for ignoring the work of other scholars in this field, such as Eastern scientific and philosophical thought as well as the Western critical tradition of Marxism. The Frankfurt school, for example, had initiated studies that sought to reconcile nature and culture (Rose 1987). Nevertheless, Merchant's contribution to feminist scholarship has been as important as it was original.

These trends in historical analysis concluded that the masculine values which evolved were due to more than male dominance in science and technology. After all, it is not *all* men who are involved in or who support the values and goals that direct these fields. But it was through male dominance at a certain stage that a pervasive mind-set developed in scientific thinking and practice, which has become analogous to present concepts of masculinity.[21] This use of control and power imagery is still practiced today in the form of military metaphors, as pointed out by Hynes (1989a), who showed how often male technologists are alluded to as "heroic men who *fight* disease, insects and drought, who *conquer* space and *crack* the genetic code" (emphasis added).

Analyzing technology in the context of theories of patriarchy and the sexual division of labor raises the question, what are the consequences of male dominance and the dominant mechanistic paradigm in the production of scientific and technological knowledge? in technical education? in jobs requiring technical skills? and on the individual level between the private and public spheres? One answer is that gender-linked value systems are created. The feminist literature uses many pairs of terms in discussing these differing values: male and female, humanitarian and technical, technical rationality and caring rationality. It speaks of research based on a scientific rationality, on the one hand, or a holistic approach, on the other. Scientific rationality is viewed as reductionism or fragmentation and the basis of the creation of the assembly line method of work (Frankel 1973; Henderson 1975; Roszak 1974).[22] A holistic and integrated approach is seen as representative of a set of values that take subjective factors into consideration and prioritize a totalistic view of problem-solving (Dolkart and Hartstock 1975; Firestone 1970).

Male values, associated with scientific rationality, are seen as synonymous with those that underlie modern technology. Rothschild (1983) finds that technology reflects such male values as conquest, dominance, rationality, and objectivity; as a consequence, women's inferiority becomes embedded in scientific and technological thinking and activities. She raises the question of whether the present links (both material and ideological) between technology, capitalism, and patriarchy can ever be liberating for women in particular and for society in general. She sees the present technological order as suppressing not only women but human- and female-identified values.

A field of research that has dealt with the consequences of scientific rationality and its values of domination and control is the feminist body of literature on the history of medical science. It points out that the development of Western medicine has had far-reaching consequences for women. A combination of scientific rationality and biomedical technologies has seriously affected many areas of women's lives, including birth control, abortion, and childbearing (Arditti 1979; Ehrenreich and

English 1979; Gordon 1977; Rich 1977). A point made repeatedly in the women's health literature is that the medical establishment in the past century has increasingly medicalized women's bodies. "Medicalization" refers to the attachment of medical labels to normal bodily functions and social issues, which implies that modern medicine has the knowledge and the tools to intervene and permits it to claim the ability to cure many problems—including social ones. For women, medicalization means defining such normal bodily functions as menstruation, pregnancy, birth, and menopause and such social issues as rape and violence as medical problems requiring medical treatment. The values of domination and control that such medicalization represents have become a pivotal issue in feminist research on the introduction of new reproductive technologies.

The feminist literature on the implications for women of male dominance and masculine values in science and technology claims that these gender-linked value systems are closely related to the detailed sexual division of labor as it developed under capitalism and during the process of socialization. Although some branches of women's studies find theories of capitalism and patriarchy too materialistic an explanation, the fact remains that the discussion of technology, women, and values is firmly placed within discussions of the division of labor by sex, which provides men and women with different experiences and perceptions of the world. It is argued that by performing separate and distinct tasks, each sex develops its own particular culture—a male and a female subculture—each with its own knowledge base, beliefs, morals, and customs. In this view, the motivating power behind the development of technology is perceived as male rationality and its desire to preserve the sexual division of labor in society. "If some groups are freed by tools and others become tied down as they operate them, different ideologies will develop between these people. While the freed people will develop ideals about activity, independence, mobility, achievement and competence, those who get tied down will need to explain and evaluate their functions" (Aas 1975, 151).

In the humanities, theories of culture are the basis for analyzing subculture.[23] The feminist analysis argues that through the development and introduction of and experience with technological innovations, different and often opposing value systems develop and/or old (often oppressing) ones are reinforced. By performing certain work functions, women have been representatives for certain cultural value sets; the same is true for men. Male and female values have become expressions of a social ideology that has contributed to hardening the division of labor between the sexes. This ideology prescribes the places of "real" women and men in the labor market.

The theme of a female subculture has been developed by Bergom-Larsson (1982), who draws up a list of characteristics detected in women's culture (based on Liljestroem 1979) which have consequences for women's mode of relating to technological development: (1) a horizontal organizational model without a leadership stratum; (2) valuations based on aesthetic, social, and religious criteria; (3) an organic conceptualization of time; (4) a multidimensional, complex conception of causality (rationality or responsibility); (5) orientation toward people instead of machines.

Louise Walden (1982) has examined the relations between male culture, female culture, and technological culture—the last defined as the dominating mentality in a society based on technology. She finds that the aims and purpose of technical work are and have been largely influenced by male culture because of male dominance in this field. She warns that in considering technological thinking, we must not confuse it with its opposite, humanistic thinking. Men and women share both modes of thinking, but it is the male perspective that prevails in the technical world as a consequence of male dominance: "Visions of the good life are prevalent in the goals and aims of female culture while the 'effective society' is more in line with male culture's goals and aims" (p. 19; my translation).

The psychologist Carol Gilligan (1982) has researched basic differences between the moral systems and criteria of men and women. She describes two ethical codes emerging from two different spheres of experience: a code based on care and responsibility for others (cf. Boman 1981), and a code based on rights, self-assertion, and individual struggle. She emphasizes that although these spheres have historically been associated with women and men respectively, both are essential to the mature development of both men and women; either code alone represents a fragmented picture of the world. As she points out, with an ethics of individual rights one might reach equality, but this is no guarantee of equity.

Similarly, Walden (1982) asserts the importance of female technicians in influencing the future of technology; through their experiences in the feminine sphere, women can counterbalance the male-rational mode of thinking. Increased numbers of women in technological fields, she believes, will have a positive influence on the aims and purposes of the technical world.[24]

This leads to the next question: do women who are now in the field of technology have a view of or perspective on technology different from that of their male counterparts? If so, do their differing value systems affect their professions' priorities?

The study of values has perhaps been most prolific in the study of women in the technological professions, especially engineering. Although some investigations concluded that an increase in the number of women was unlikely to "disturb" the value system of the engineering profession, others began to show gender differences. For example, Berner (1975) found that twice as many girls as boys said that they started a technical education because it would give them an opportunity to improve the environment. This is similar to the findings of Elin Kvande (1982), who concluded from her study of female engineering students in Norway that women's technological values are different from men's. In her opinion, women as a group have much to contribute to the humanization of technology. She attributes the presence of woman-specific values to the socialization process, where communication with and responsibility for other people play a large role. She found that efficiency and technological rationality were not valued as highly by female engineering students as by their male colleagues.

A Swedish study (Walden 1982) concludes, however, that women who work in the natural sciences share many of the same values as men who work in the natural sciences, and that there are greater differences in values between natural scientists and humanists than there are between women and men within the same discipline.[25]

When Lauritzen (1990) looked at the gender divisions in the natural and technical sciences in Denmark, in an attempt to understand why there were so few women, she found differences within disciplines as to where women were choosing to work and what they believed to be exciting and important areas.[26] In Denmark today, very few women can be found working and studying in university departments in mathematics and physics; there are almost none in the computer sciences; and the number of new female students in these fields is dropping.[27] Lauritzen attributes this to the dominance of masculine values in science and technology.

Utopian Alternatives

It should be noted that not all feminist writings about technological development have been negative. Optimism and the positive potential of technology can be found in the feminist utopian literature that gained attention in the 1970s. Men's science fiction has been criticized as not only conservative but also reactionary in that it tends to show society becoming infused with ever more sophisticated technology (Rose 1986). In contrast, the feminist science fiction that emerged offered the potential for new utopian societies. Although it spans a wide range of visions, there is common agreement in this literature on at least one area: a general theme is major changes in the built environment whereby utopian housing accommodates extended families, has provisions for child care, and stimulates personal contacts.

The most creative visions have been in the focus of this literature on reproductive technology, which I see as an exercise in creative visualization for alternative approaches to women's role in pregnancy and birth. In fact, several authors have explored the potential for female liberation through reproductive technology, offering futuristic forecasts that look favorably upon such reproductive technologies as artificial insemination, sperm banks, ex utero fertilization (test-tube babies), surrogate motherhood; genetic screening, amniocentesis, and in vitro fetal development (artificial wombs).

Some feminist theorists and writers even propose these technologies as *prerequisites* for female freedom. Shulamith Firestone, in *The Dialectic of Sex* (1970), suggests that reproductive technology can free women from the "tyranny of reproduction" and the "barbaric" character of pregnancy. She envisions a mechanical womb and presents a utopia that promises women the continuation of the species independent of men. The women in Joanna Russ's utopia (1975) live in and with high technology. As there are no men, ova fusion and parthenogenesis have been developed as alternative modes of reproduction. Marge Piercy, in *Woman on the Edge of Time* (1976), fantasizes a postgendered society where children develop in a "birthing house" and each child is assigned three mothers. Men not only qualify as "mothers" but have been treated with hormones so that they are capable of breastfeeding and thus of nurturing and bonding with the infant in a way that is not biologically possible today.

Ultimately, many of these scenarios would isolate and alienate women from men altogether. They *assume* (without offering an explanation of how) that women will control these technologies. The argument is that if women control the methods of reproduction (with little or no dependence on men), they will control their fertility and, in turn, their lives. This control would expand to encompass societal issues such as education and work conditions. On the basis of this argument, one could even go so far as to project an end to discrimination in the job market as the result of perfect planning and only wanted pregnancies. That sort of optimism is more the exception than the rule, however. More often, critical feminists argue that new reproductive technology will offer the medical establishment opportunity to assert even more control over women's bodies.

I appreciate the utopian scenarios for their attempt to open new ways of thinking about reproduction and women's role in it; however, I find problems with them because the material basis of women's role in production and reproduction is largely ignored and thus the way in which such visions of society might be supported is not developed.

Implications for Feminist Research and Assessment
This chapter presents the feminist scholarship on technological development as an introduction to a feminist approach to TA. This sequence is important in that I view each of various approaches to TA as a reflection of a particular understanding of the role and influence of technology in society.

Feminist studies are the work of an interdisciplinary

community. This means that feminist studies of women and technology are done on different levels of analysis (individual, group, organization, society) and address research questions of various kinds (epistemological, cultural, societal, economic, psychological). This also means that there is no one accepted theory of women's oppression and no single approach to technological development on which to build a feminist perspective on TA.

I find the implications for building a feminist approach to TA/MTA to be the further development of the themes that have emerged from feminist studies of technological development: systems of domination and control; division of labor; values. All three themes must be seen in light of the initial task of feminist studies, which is to make visible through concrete examples the role and accomplishments of women.

By introducing gender, feminist studies enhanced the radical science analysis of science and technology that was prevalent in the 1970s. In this way, feminist studies contributed to the analysis of science and technology as part of a system of domination. The feminist analysis of technological development regards technology as a tool for maintaining the oppression of women in society, on the labor market, and at home. The argument that a change in any one part of the culture will be accompanied by changes in other parts (Aas 1975) presents a challenge for TA.

From a feminist perspective, domination and oppression are key factors in the study of technological development and essential concepts in a feminist analysis of TA. Some professions, social classes, and groups are seen to have the power to press forward the development of that technology which can benefit their personal or collective interests, without regard for detrimental effects on others. This means that power, control, and oppression are intimately connected with and expressed through technological development.[28] In other words, technology creates ad-

vantages for some and disadvantages for others. Social relations act through technology and techniques, which in
turn reinforce social relations. Where those social relations are oppressive, this mechanism acts as a vicious cy-
cle of oppression.

I have found the theories of patriarchy in the critical
feminist tradition appropriate for studying technological
development in relation to TA. The further development
of the analysis of the division of labor by sex can be particularly useful in providing an understanding of why
men and women relate to technology in different ways.
Capitalism and patriarchy are seen in an interplay with
technology within the same period of history, an interplay pivotal in the development of the technology we
have today and its effects on women.

Feminist theories that analyze capitalism and patriarchy as two separate spheres take for granted that the
primary unit of patriarchal relations is the family. But
this view fails to bring into focus the character and degree of women's specific oppression *as* women outside the
family. For this reason, I did not find these theories useful
in identifying and analyzing the implications for TA of
women's specific oppression in the two sectors I studied,
the clerical and health care sectors.

I have found evidence that points to a deterioration of
women's situation with the rise of capitalism. Through
the development of capitalism the division of labor by sex
became more specialized and hierarchical. The differences between men's and women's roles became wider
and more distinct and developed a material base. Under
capitalism women's work was marginalized (keeping
both status and wages low), and technology played an important role. Chapter 7 demonstrates how rapidly the
horizontal division of labor developed to make room for
women in the previously male-dominated clerical sector.
This was followed by the rapid development of a new vertical division of labor that kept women at the bottom.

A temporal division, the increase in part-time work for women, has limited their career potential on the labor market; new technology making it possible for women to work at home has influenced the geographic division of labor. In the health care sector the professional knowledge and status of nurses and midwives as traditional female healers has eroded over time, and medical technology has been a recent contribution to this development.

Although capitalism has not benefited all men equally, it has affected the social relations between the sexes—both on the labor market and in the domestic sphere—and technology has played a role in these dynamics. A relevant point made by Hartsock (1983) is that masculinity has been attained through opposition to daily life: men escape from the female world of the household to the masculine world of public life—a point worth remembering in assessing the effect of technology on women.[29]

Through an analysis of values, feminist scholars have given the study of technological change a new dimension by analyzing the consequences of male dominance in science and technology. The underrepresentation of women in technological professions as well as in TA research and practice is a reflection of asymmetric power relations between the sexes. Feminists claim that technology embodies male social values and male perceptions of problems, and offers male solutions. It follows that male-biased technologies have a differentiated impact on men and women, and that this should be a consideration in TA/MTA.

In much of the feminist literature, the discussions of values are associated with the sexual division of labor, but the implications for research are problems of definition and levels of analysis. For example, in many of these discussions "male values" are said to be built into modern science and technology, without any explanation of what is meant. The level of analysis ranges from values associated with the epistemology of modern science to values that women develop during the execution of their daily chores. I find the reason for the confusion and vagueness is that often values as such are not the focus of study but are dealt with as relative to and sometimes even by-products of established and changing knowledge, norms, ethics, and material goods.

In the critical feminist literature on technology the discussion of values, based on theories of capitalism and patriarchy, elaborates the inherent values of both. The relevance of this argument for TA is that it holds true for all groups that have no control over the development or implementation of technology, as some groups provide the tools of control while others are subject to control through technology.

Summary

The purpose of this chapter has been to construct a theoretical understanding upon which a critical feminist approach to TA can develop. In presenting the major trends in feminist research on women and technology, I have emphasized the important part played by knowledge interests, which can be found in the implicit and explicit theories underlying TA as it is practiced today.

Three contributions that feminist research can make to the further development of TA are the analysis of science and technology as part of a system of domination, the further development of the division-of-labor analysis, and an analysis of values. In the feminist analysis, values are seen as a form of social ideology that has contributed to maintaining the division of labor between the sexes by acting as a guide to what "appropriate" male and female work should be. Feminist research proposes that as a social category, gender is both male and female, allowing men and women the possibility of developing their feminine and masculine sides.

6
A Feminist Approach to Assessment

It is less important to the goals of technology assessment to determine whether technology has been built upon scientific rationality and male dominance than to ask whether there is any possibility for science, technology, and policy research to grow and change over time.

The justification for analyzing and presenting any specific approach to TA should be its ability to contribute insights that can be useful for TA in general. In the emancipatory tradition of critical studies, concerned with freedom and the problems of self-liberation, the purpose is to make visible those factors that support or hinder democratic principles. What this means in practice is that by involving different social groups in TA, we may better recognize future impacts and generate more desirable options. Technology, seen as a social process, is something that can be influenced by social forces. I argue that the feminist literature on technological development can contribute to the further development of TA.

I have analyzed existing resources in an attempt to draw out from this body of knowledge the lessons that can be applied to the development of a critical TA. This chapter presents the feminist scholarship on TA and how it relates to nonfeminist research. It concludes with what I consider a preliminary list of elements for assessment that lives up to critical and feminist demands.

The Importance of a Feminist Approach

Judy Smith (1981) identifies two good reasons for developing a feminist approach to TA: first, women often feel that technology is not something they can control; second, the appropriate technology and alternative energy movements are directed by men. I find both reasons applicable to people or groups who are not part of development or decision-making. Better directed technological development requires an assessment that develops according to people's needs. Achieving this is not a simple task. Smith illustrates how so-called appropriate technology can affect women. For example, if we use less energy, women might have to spend more time on home maintenance and would have less time for other things. She is, however, cautious: "Determining what would make a technology appropriate from a feminist perspective will be a complex task, for some technologies have actually expanded women's role options while others have restricted them; moreover, some technologies are so threatening to women that they should be completely eliminated" (Smith 1981, 20–21).

Perhaps all TA should begin by asking, what effects (if any) will this have on women? The evaluation of all technological developments can be structured with focus on women's social interaction, even those that initially seem to have little to do with women's lives. One example is the introduction of the bicycle. It is hard to believe today that women's bike riding was discouraged (by bottles and insults thrown their way); in some Eastern cultures it is still a cultural taboo (Kramarae 1988).

TA can become a valuable tool in monitoring the effects of technological change on women's economic and social roles. Studies suggest that new technologies are affecting precisely those areas of work in which large numbers of women are employed (Zmroczek and Henwood 1983).

> One of the central issues in the technology debate as far as women are concerned is that of their vulnerability to the changes that are taking place. A 1983 ILO [International Labor Office] study suggests that although new technologies can have a more or less beneficial effect on employment, skills, and work organization in general terms, it is clear that, at least in the short term, they are going to have a substantial impact on women who are generally found in those occupations that are most likely to undergo change in the use of new technology, being concentrated in these "at risk" jobs to a far greater extent than men. [Greve 1987, 38]

A TA that is appropriate for women would attempt to make women's contributions and women's needs visible to society—not only to the male members of society but to the female as well. It is not enough for policy-makers to be made aware of women's needs; women must look out for their own interests, and making their needs visible is a means of making all women aware of the role technology plays in their lives. It is important for women to understand how technology affects them and their lives, and how they can affect technology. The very definition of TA links it to policy-making. It is important that women, as a potential influence in directing technological development, play a part in policy-making.

Educating and motivating women to become involved in TA is not easy, however. Bose (1988) relates the problems of teaching a course on women and technology. She reports that her students, especially those from the hard sciences, have trouble understanding the relevance of a feminist analysis, a fact she attributes to their lack of training in critical analysis. Evidently, it takes them weeks to understand that biology, engineering, physics, and so on are not objective facts but rather perspectives, approaches, or paradigms themselves.[1]

Two Feminist Models
The feminist literature has dealt only briefly with issues of TA, mainly as a critique of existing methods that lack a sex/gender analysis. A few authors, however, have attempted to address the issue (Bruce and Adams 1989; Kirejczyk 1988; Koch and Morgall 1987; Kolmos 1989; Smith 1981), and their contributions have been meaningful, especially in synthesizing feminist literature.

I offer here two examples of feminist approaches to TA, which I have chosen for their thoroughness and because they attempt to build TA models. The first comes from the work of Corlann Gee Bush (1983), who presents a general approach; the second example is from Patricia Hynes (1987), who specifically addresses reproductive technology.

Corlann Gee Bush
In the early 1980s, Bush (1981) developed what she called the Feminist Technology Assessment Wheel, which presents three levels of effects that can be scored for their degree of desirability.[2] Used extensively in women's studies, it offers an innovative way to assess a given technological change, showing how multiple effects interact. Some years later, she developed a detailed, comprehensive feminist approach to TA (Bush 1983) to address all types of technology. I present it here in brief, using her terminology.

Bush defines technology as a form of human cultural activity that applies the principles of science and mechanics to the solution of problems. Her definition includes the resources, tools, processes, personnel, and systems developed to perform tasks and to create immediate particular and personal or competitive advantages in a given ecological, economic, and social context.

She bases her assessment model on two key concepts: technology myths and the process of "unthink." She assumes that "myths associated with technology" exist and affect women in a negative way. These "myths" that discriminate against women can be eliminated through the method of "unthink," which is similar to consciousness raising as practiced in the women's movement. Given that women's thoughts and consciousness are strongly bound to a patriarchal culture and to patriarchal interests, "unthinking" is a process that challenges an accepted truth and sees it as a myth servicing the interests of some but not all. Bush considers "unthink" an activity that can be a precondition for all social movement and change.

Bush analyzes the assumptions underlying myths of technology, which she claims are popular opinions held by large groups of politicians and experts, and condenses these assumptions into three concepts: tool, threat, and triumph. To unthink the myth of technology as tool—that is, not good or bad but merely neutral—is perhaps the hardest process of the three, for this myth is deeply ingrained in our value system. She uses the example of the gun, which *could* be considered a neutral tool, as it can be used both to kill a person for revenge and to shoot a bird for dinner. But this view, she argues, does not grasp the collective significance of the technology in question, for tools and technologies have a valence, or bias. They are charged and tend "to seek out or fit in with certain social norms or disturb others." A gun looked upon in this light is seen to be designed exclusively for killing in a way that previously used hammers, knives, and other tools were not.

Similarly, Bush sets out to unthink the myth of technology as the triumph of human civilization, as tantamount to human progress.[3] It is the belief that technology can solve all problems, including social ones. To deal with the complexity of this myth is to acknowledge that it has a core of truth—that is, much technology *has* improved the human condition—but at the same time to recognize the tremendous problems that technology has created for our society. She sees the third and opposing myth, technology as threat, as equally overstated: for example, in the way some environmental organizations react to any modern use of technology.

Bush argues that such polarized thinking will not serve the best interests of society. It will become clear, she claims, that if we are to continue the process of unthinking myths, we cannot evaluate technology in a vacuum, or by considering only immediate effects. Consequently, she suggests that we should conceive of technology as "an organized system of interactions that utilizes tools and involves techniques for the performance of tasks and the accomplishment of objectives." She proposes that technologies operate within a context, that social messages—including those that influence the situation of groups such as women—are at work.

Bush identifies four contexts in which technology exists: the *design or development context*, including the decisions, personnel, processes, and systems necessary to create tools and techniques from raw material; the *user context*, including the motivations, intentions, advantages, and adjustments called into play by the use of particular techniques or tools; the *environmental context*, including the nonspecific physical surroundings in which a technology is developed and used; the *cultural context*, including the norms, values, myths, aspirations, laws, and interactions of the society of which the tool or technique is a part. Traditionally, she points out, the main interest has been the first of these, the developmental context, because of the preference of civilized man to think of himself as creator and conqueror of the natural world. The ecological crisis has made it necessary to think more carefully about our dependence on the natural world surrounding us and, as Bush puts it, "to unthink the arrogance of our assumption that we are separate from and

superior to nature." Bush presents as an example an attempt by the Montana Women and Technology Project to
do environmental impact analyses of specific technologies
by producing sex-role impact reports that could improve
our knowledge of cultural and social consequences. To ob-
tain an equity analysis of new technology, Bush proposes
that risks and benefits be listed and evaluated within
each of the contexts mentioned. This would require a new
definition of technology that includes both women and facilities in equity analyses.

Bush stresses the virtue of a new definition that incorporates the concept of advantage, showing that technologies are accepted or developed because people find advantages connected with their use. Such a definition makes it
possible to look for aspects or consequences of technologies that benefit some and disadvantage others. In other
words, it has the potential for a conflict-oriented approach to TA, in line with the feminist analysis of
women's social and cultural position as inferior to men's
and as subject to men.

Bush views technology as an equity issue. She points
out that all technologies exist in social contexts, which
they influence—one way or another—to the advantage or
disadvantage of women. An understanding of the context
in which technology operates is necessary in order to understand how technology influences and affects our
world. Bush concludes that society will be transformed
by new technology; therefore, feminists must work to
transform society to make technology equitable.

Patricia Hynes
Another explicit attempt to build a TA model using a feminist approach comes from Patricia Hynes (1987). Her
point of departure is *Silent Spring* by Rachel Carson
(1962), which, she believes, holds paradigmatic value for
the international feminist movement against new reproductive technology.[4] Hynes draws on the work done in en-

vironmental protection to develop similar guidelines for the protection of the reproductive rights of women. She proposes using already established policy and protective laws, and relating them to the new field of reproductive technology. She suggests that the ideas and analysis be worked into (1) policy and laws and (2) a feminist critique of technology that she views as "high-tech" subjugation of women.

Hynes relies on the analogy between women and the environment because, first, women and nature are both the playground of men's scientific tinkering and manipulation; therefore, their rights are least and last protected. Second, women and nature share a common philosophical footing: a conviction of the right to live unendangered by our society.

Hynes's main criticism of reproductive technologies is that though they are essentially experimental, they are promoted as cure; women are exposed to "drift."[5] She believes that the media perpetuate the myth of fulfillment through motherhood, anesthetizing the deeper questions of freedom of choice and motivation of choice. She sees the tension of feminism in the fact that women live in a man's world while trying to create a woman's world. She relates this effort to "two-sights seeing," which looks near (short term) and far (long term). She describes Carson as farsighted in that by looking backward and forward in time, she considered the implications of the widespread application of synthetic chemicals into the ecosystem. Inspired by Carson's work, Hynes has built the model for a feminist TA (see Table 3), which shows how the risks and benefits of a given technology can be compared with those of an alternative.

Hynes takes up the issue of what she calls the "existential risk" of new reproductive technologies, such as treatments for infertility, and presents the "metaphysical risks to women." First, experimentation on women's

Table 3
Hynes's Model for a Feminist TA

Benefit	Method	Risk
Enable infertile women to bear children	In vitro fertilization (IVF)	Adverse effects from hormones Trauma to ovary Risks from anesthesia with repeated operations Risks from procedures for monitoring IVF Potential damage to uterus Risk of ectopic pregnancy
Enable infertile women to bear children Reduce infertility permanently Create additional health benefits	Research the industrial, environmental, and medically induced causes of infertility Recommend reducing exposure to chemicals and technologies identified to cause infertility and taking them off the market Quantitate percentage change in fertility expected	"0" risk to women Costs to industry of replacing chemicals that cause infertility and modifying workplace exposure offset by savings in insurance from lessened liability

Source: Hynes 1987, 197. Reprinted by kind permission of the author.

bodies without full knowledge of the effects reinforces the valuelessness and expendability of women.[6] Second, the medical fantasy of unlimited technocratic control over women's procreative powers is legitimized. Third, women are reduced to sources of eggs, embryos, and wombs, further obliterating their value as autonomous beings. Much as wetlands were once treated as waste-lands to dredge and fill, women become bodies to dredge and fill, useful only as sites for medical engineering.[7] Fourth, a false sense of safety and success is generated when, in fact, technologies create greater risk of infertility because they sidetrack society from recognizing its predominant causes and blunt any protest against exposure to chemicals, industrial products, and medical practices that cause sterility.

Hynes examines the flourishing worldwide legislation that is beginning to focus on commercializing surrogacy, regularizing the status of offspring, controlling the traffic in eggs and sperm, and limiting experimentation on embryos. The concerns addressed by such legislation are the commercialization of wombs (although not the traffic in women), experimentation on embryos, and crass profiteering in eggs, embryos, and wombs. Her criticism is that these concerns do not take into consideration the reduction of women to bodily parts and reproductive resources.

Hynes sees the issues to be included in a woman-specific model of TA as having technical/medical, social/legal, and cultural aspects. In other words, her approach to TA views technology in a social context of conflicting interests.

Discussion
The models presented by Bush and Hynes contain some very important issues that can contribute to the further development of TA. There are, however, certain problems with both approaches.

Bush builds her model around what she calls the four contexts and emphasizes that the feminist viewpoint becomes clearest within the "cultural context." For me, this is much too narrow in scope; it is as if sex roles were to be found only in the cultural context. I believe that all four contexts need a feminist perspective. There are various stages of technological development in which the social meanings of technology are being constructed and reconstructed. It is a contradiction to say that technology is an equity issue and then propose that TA concentrate on the cultural context more than on the other three. It is not only through culture that inequality is bred. Further, to her four contexts I would add a fifth, the socioeconomic context, which would include the social and material factors influencing development, dissemination, and end-user conditions.

I find Bush's use of the concept of "myth" problematic, confusing myth with popular perception. For example, is the popular belief in technology as progress really a myth: that is, an expression of the collective unconscious? There has always been public protest to technology in one form or another, more visible at certain times in history than at others.

Bush's major contribution to the field of TA, in my view, is her emphasis on the importance of developing strategies for changes in social relations.

Although Hynes has not forgotten the material factors, I find problems in her approach as well. Her analogy of pesticides and IVF does not hold. By presenting women as nature and comparing them to the wetlands of Rachel Carson's book (bodies to be "dredged and filled"), she tends to reduce women to a piece of nature to be preserved.

Most of the points she takes up are not "woman-specific" but can be generalized to any TA that can be seen as an advantage—even though that is not the intent of her argument. She does examine relevant issues such as technological fixes; the belief in technological progress; the cases of iatrogenesis; false cost-benefit calculation; conflicts of interest; the need to include users in TA; the practice of experimentation on humans; the lack of a holistic perception of the human body in modern medicine; the commercialization of body parts. But though I regard her model as a good start, it does not take into account the sociological and psychological aspects of infertility.

I find Hynes's major contributions to be her adaptation of the concept of "drift" (effects beyond the area to which treatment is directed); her exposure of the promotion of techniques and procedures as "cures" when they are actually experiments (this was the case of the introduction of IVF in Denmark; Koch and Morgall 1987) and when the reasons for "success" are often unknown; her proposal for "two-sights seeing," near and far, since analyzing short-term and long-term effects is essential; and her insistence on the public's right to information.

Her contribution to a TA that specifically assesses reproduction includes dispelling the myth of fulfillment through motherhood, and promoting legislative controls over new reproductive technology (every other industry has such controls, so why not biotechnology?).

A Focused Critique of TA

I have already presented a general critique of TA, as perceived by its proponents (see Chapter 4). At this point I want to offer a more focused critique, using a critical and feminist perspective.

As mentioned before, feminist literature dealing specifically with TA is sparse. What I present here should not be considered a feminist consensus but rather my synthesis of the resources summarized so far—feminist theory, feminist scholarship on technology, a feminist approach to TA—and one more source: namely, nonfeminist research. Following this, I take up the relationship between the feminist critique and that of other social movements; a feminist critique of TA's approach, theories, and methods; and the specific demands and major difficulties of a critical feminist approach. My purpose is to develop a basis from which to draw criteria for a critical TA and MTA.

This focused critique is aimed at institutionalized TA, since this is the primary source of assessment that affects public policy and, therefore, women as a group; however, the critique is often applicable to much of non-institutionalized TA as well.

Nonfeminist Theories
I consider nonfeminist theories a source of inspiration for building a critical feminist critique of TA. As mentioned in the preceding chapter, in the 1960s and 1970s the theories and methods of critical social science developed parallel to social movements and, in fact, inspired them theoretically. Although it is beyond the scope of this book to do justice to every one of these trends, a summary of the discussions on technological development is necessary to the development of my critique.

A starting point for these discussions is the claim that technological determinism as theory is part of the dominant research approach in science today.[8] In fact, much of the mainstream literature points to a belief that technology itself determines the organization of work (MacKenzie and Wajcman 1987). This is unfortunate, because although this body of research is very large, it is not in this research tradition to address the most basic question when assessing technology that affects women: that is, what role does it play in perpetuating inequalities in society?

Several theories developing in 1970s research addressed issues of technology and dominance: for example, in the labor process debate and in social constructionist and feminist studies. A body of research, mainly Marxist in origin, developed under the name of labor process theory. The labor process debate provided an invaluable historical analysis of how and why technology developed as a controlling rather than liberating factor in the workplace. This theory examines the role that capitalism has played in technology development and views the degradation of work as central to understanding the functioning of modern capitalist societies. How and to what extent technological change has affected human consciousness and behavior cannot be explained either by technology itself or by purely utilitarian or material factors. History contains countless examples of technology that failed to infuse itself into the social consciousness of a people and to generate change in the social order.

In this view, control over the labor process finds expression in the concentration of knowledge, in the tools of production, and at the price of the workers' qualifications and control. Technology is understood as developing through a society characterized by inequalities between individuals and groups; therefore, it cannot be neutral. Technology is not regarded as a determining factor, but seen within the context of a market economy that has the possibility of being influenced by noneconomic factors.

Technology is regarded as a social process, technological change as a process of human activities and therefore something that can be controlled. The role played by different social forces is strongly emphasized, thus focusing the analysis on the relationship between actors in various social contexts. Technology can be redirected only through a confrontation between various interest groups. The goal is to uncover the power interests and to localize the obstacles that hinder a democratic development of production. Only after having accomplished this can a new direction for technological development be formulated. Empirical evidence that technology has been used as a mechanism to regulate and guide operations and systems has made control the key variable in this analysis. In areas of production and reproduction, the links between technology and control are present, although often complex and not always obvious.

Characteristic of the labor process debate is its practice of seeing capital not only as an economic category but as a relationship between human beings. What I consider major contributions in this area include the analysis of the division of labor and scientific management by Braverman (1974); the historical analysis of control systems in the workplace by Edwards (1979); and the various contributions of David Noble (1977, 1979) on social choice in technological development. Noble's historical analyses of technology as a reflection of existing social relations and of technology's role in mediating control in the labor process are major contributions.

The strength of this body of knowledge lies in its critique of technological determinism and its emphasis on the social and economic aspects of technological development. The major weaknesses of the labor process analysis are, first, that it is gender blind and, second, that it focuses exclusively on production.

Social constructionist analysis, in its attempt to study the effects that society has on technology, poses the question, what has shaped the technology that is having the effects?[9] A classic example is Noble's work on social choice in machine design (1979). Using a detailed step-by-step analysis, he found that a major goal of automation was to secure managerial power by shifting control from the shop floor to the central office. He made an important contribution by showing that automation did not have to proceed the way it did; the form it took was the result of deliberate selection among social and economic choices, made by those who had the power to choose. Noble emphasizes that one can understand technical choices only by paying attention to the conflictual relations of production within which automation takes place. He argues that science shapes technology but that science itself is affected by the society in which it is conducted.

Institutionalized TA evaluates the effects of technology according to its impact on society. From this perspective, it is paramount to look at what has shaped the technology that is having the effect (MacKenzie and Wajcman 1987). The question should be what effect society has on technology, a point that David Noble has discussed at length. "There is always a range of possibilities or alternatives that are delimited over time—as some are selected and others denied—by the social choices of those with the power to choose, choices which reflect their intentions, ideology, social position, and relations with other people in society. In short technology bears the social 'imprint' of its authors" (Noble 1979, 18–19).

The belief that technology progresses and that negative consequences for work organization and occupational health are immutable are sentiments found in the literature of technological determinism. It is this body of work that provokes social constructionists to ask: What if technological determinism is wrong? What if the "effects" on work are deliberately (or accidentally) built into the design? What if the technology could be designed differently? In my own research I have asked, what do the answers to these questions mean for women?

Links to Other Social Movements
I consider a feminist approach to TA as an extension and further elaboration of the approach taken by the "new social movements" of the 1970s and 1980s, particularly the environmental movement (Hynes 1987, 1989b). I see a close relationship between the two and find similarities that form a critique of technological development in general and TA in particular. In many ways, there are similarities between the women's movement and other social movements in their approach to theoretical, methodological, and strategic considerations: for example, the desire for participatory politics and democratic culture in response to technological development.

Similar theoretical groundings can be found in the movements' emancipatory approach to TA, based on the critical research tradition that advocates a theory and method intended to promote political consciousness and self-actualization. To convert these characteristics into strategy, the research of the social movements advocates empowerment and self-help. The critical tradition, however, is only one of many non-institutionalized theoretical approaches to TA. The approaches taken by social movements, pressure groups, and academia are not always critical and can all be criticized for ignoring gender.

A Critical Feminist Critique of TA
Interpreted from a feminist perspective, the fact that the methods presented in Chapter 3 did not allow for the option of total rejection means that the most frequently used methods encourage consensus and adaptation. By not including the option to reject new or abolish established technology, institutionalized TA appears to support and encourage innovations rather than questioning them. In other words, TA appears to be quality control rather than a critical challenge. In practice, this approach encourages adaptation and the maintenance of the status quo rather than a search for alternatives. In contrast, a critical feminist approach emphasizes conflict and tension and a TA that provides methods for dealing with both.

One difference between the social movements' and the feminists' approaches to TA is their proposed focus for assessment. Whereas social movements represent an emancipatory approach that emphasizes the democratic process in TA, a feminist approach focuses on issues of dominance and the hierarchial relations in society.

If, as Noble says, technology bears the imprint of its authors, the same can be said for TA. For example, Bruce and Adams (1989) point out that nonfeminist studies of technology designed to be used by women fail to capture both the way women actually feel about the technology and the way they foresee the future of this development in regard to their own lives. Therefore, a feminist critique of TA is concerned not only with the technology itself but also with theories and methods of assessment that can oppress women. A gender-specific example of bad TA, taken from the work of Raymond (1989), will serve to illustrate that risk-benefit calculations can be biased against women.

In the United States there has been a debate concerning the beneficial uses of fetal tissue. Victims of Parkinson's and Huntington's diseases have been shown to benefit from treatment using brain tissue obtained from aborted fetuses. This has caused an ethical dilemma for doctors and the Catholic Church, who see in such treatments a risk of abortion abuse by women. Feminists, on the other hand, perceive that the real ethical problem is the greater risk that this technology could potentially abuse women, in that doctors who are concerned only with the promise of a new surgical frontier might encourage (even pressure) women to participate.

What is the risk and for whom? This is the real question. To date, the ethical considerations of new reproductive technologies have centered on the commercialization aspect and its impact on the cheapening of life, on controlling experimentation on fetuses, on patents in reproductive medicine, and on paternity. Until now, the risk to and benefit for the fetus, the doctor, and the father have been the focus of concern, while the major health and welfare impacts of these technologies on women have been ignored (Raymond 1989).

Opposition to new technology is often labeled protest against progress; this is the argument when assessment methods that have no theoretical anchor are used. Since most institutionalized TA lacks explicit theoretical grounding, these methods often neutralize TA by ignoring the conflicts and contradictions in society. Technology is seen as something that can be integrated, given time, into society.

Ratcliff (1989) illustrates this problem in her discussion of physician as assessors of medical technology. Doctors are taught to be competent but not critical users of the latest medical innovations. On the whole they are biased by their education in favor of high-tech treatment. As assessors, they possess what Ratcliff calls an "unsophisticated training in research methodology." She explains this as a fault in their basic training in the natural sciences, which does not usually include statistics and research methodology, let alone social theory. This leaves doctors ill equipped to evaluate the often confusing and conflicting literature relevant to medical technology. Its sheer volume is overwhelming, putting doctors at the mercy of industry sources for information on specific technologies (McKinlay 1981; Waldron 1977). "In a study of one drug, sales representatives from pharmaceutical companies were found to be the first source of information for half of the doctors" (Ratcliff 1989, 187).

Another problem with atheoretical methods is that they often view assessment as empirical; that is, they see assessment as a study of the clash between existing social/cultural values and the social reality created by technology. This view is backed by a belief in technology as progress and a conviction that the problem facing technological development is culture lag.[10] The goal of these approaches is to soften the "social impact" and thus minimize the culture lag. The result of delaying the moment of public involvement in discussions of developing technology is that the assessment often begins with the finished product. Therefore, the existing technology—assumed to be a given—determines the limits of the assessment,

This approach neglects vital questions such as need. The case of the ultrasound scanning of pregnant women in Denmark illustrates this point (Koch and Morgall 1987). The Danish assessment limited itself to evaluating the optimal use of the technology; it never asked the important question, do we need this technology? Or, more specifically, do all pregnant women need this technology? When the entry point for a technology is not need, then we may never ask whether there are better or equally good alternatives. And, perhaps just as important, we have no chance to direct the social and research development toward our needs. If TA is to be used as an instrument for research policy in society, the basis must be an outline of the needs of that society.

The Demands and Difficulties of a Feminist Approach
The way to begin an assessment is to focus on a "problem" or "need," as defined by either society in general or the affected group. Proactive need assessment is considered a preferred form of TA by those with a critical approach to technological development. It begins with description and evaluation of a problem in order to initiate a process that will contribute to a solution. If it is decided that the best solution is a technological solution, then both technical and social requirements for that technology can be made and assessed.

I agree with this procedure in principle—but is this demand on TA realistic? It is not always possible to determine what the needs of society (or of specific groups such as women) really are, or what technology is necessary to fill even a recognized need.[11] A critical feminist approach to TA would argue that assessment should focus on various alternative solutions, rather than on a particular technology. Assessment that begins with a problem is more likely to open the way for alternatives than assessment of one technology (product or effect assessment), which closes the door on alternatives. And this form of TA should ideally assess not only the use of technology but also expectations for and consequences of it in the broadest possible terms: that is, taking into account all interests—not only economic but social and individual, not only current but future. The question still remains, is this possible?

A way of framing the assessment in another context is to see TA as either "goal-directed" or "exploratory," a suggestion made by Bruce and Adams (1989). They define a goal-directed assessment as one that compares the likely consequences of proceeding in one direction of technological change with those of proceeding in another (for example, in choosing the site of a nuclear power station). Exploratory TA is speculative; it considers the range and desirability of the impacts, in the longer and shorter term, of a new technology (for example, interactive video). Bruce and Adams point out that it is within the exploratory approach that an attempt to elicit impact statements about gender potential can be sought.

One problem must be addressed: although there is widespread agreement that TA should be multidisciplinary, it is often difficult for interdisciplinary groups to work together even when they are in basic agreement on the substance of an assessment. It is what Launsoe and Rieper (1987) call the problem of "paradigm differences" between the various disciplines; they point out that paradigms are part of the researchers' intellectual as well as emotional makeup.[12] "Cooperation" can result in conflict when different disciplines are required to work together.[13] Disagreement can arise over such basic questions as how to define the research question, what theoretical models and reference framework to use, and what the methodological considerations are.

A major criticism made by FINRRAGE is of what it perceives as the unwillingness of industries and governments to stop certain technological developments. As one of the groups that advocate abolishing certain technologies altogether, it objects that when its spokespersons have exposed the actual as well as the potential harm of certain innovations and have suggested a total ban, they have always been challenged by either industry, the medical profession, or the government with the question, but what is the alternative? FINRRAGE argues that this question shifts the responsibility of proof to the critics and blames them for the situation that existed before the technology was developed. As Hynes (1989a) argues, an alternative solution does not have to be offered in order for a problem to be recognized.

Nevertheless, although the limits are acknowledged, a key concept of an appropriate TA using a feminist approach *is* the search for alternatives. If there is a range of possibilities when developing a technology, there must also be a range of solutions to a particular problem, one (or more) of which may be technological. There already exist mechanisms for controlling technology, and there is always the option for the government to step in and remove decisions about the control of technology from the private (in this case also professional) to the public domain.

A further difficulty with a feminist approach is ensuring that women, their roles and needs, become visible in TA. Hynes (1989a) found that assessments of the environmental impact of the Western birth control methods introduced by international aid agencies in developing countries, and of the American Fertility Society's position on the ethics of the new reproductive technologies and surrogacy, only superficially consider the physical and social reality of women. Moreover, Bruce and Adams (1989), on the basis of their experience in doing feminist TA, report the difficulty of *involving* women. In their view, the major problem is to devise techniques and methods for critical appraisal of new technologies (especially those whose applications are unclear) for people who typically have been disfranchised of thinking and speaking about the role of technology in everyday life. This applies to women especially but to other social groups as well.

Where I Stand

Contrary to many feminist authors, I do not see bringing more women into the fields of science and technology as the most urgent priority in influencing technological development; rather, I see that as a long-term strategy. In the short term, because of the urgency of certain policy decisions, I see an immediate need to argue for a more active role for women in decision-making. I therefore propose that equity in the assessment and management of technology would itself be the most urgent technological change.

I have attempted to develop a critical TA using a feminist *approach*, which I distinguish from a feminist TA. The distinction as I see it is that a feminist TA takes women and their position in society as the basis for analysis, making the assessment dependent on a specific theory of women's oppression and thus theoretically viewing patriarchy as separate from capitalism. I advocate that TA in general, as well as a feminist approach to it, should be based on theories of technology and society that assess not the technology (the end product) exclusively or the women (the end users) exclusively but technological development in its historical and material context. I view gender characteristics as socially constructed and therefore subject to material and ideological transformation. This approach places the focus of analysis on the dynamics of the social process, women's role in or absence from it, and what a given development will mean for women's lives. It allows for a more holistic understanding of all the contributing factors rather than focusing exclusively on one. This approach has roots in the critical feminist tradition, which does *not* view patriarchy as something separate and distinct from capitalism but rather sees capitalism as being structured along gender lines.

Gender differences must be a central element in TA. This is particularly important when building on existing theories, keeping the situation for women and men visible. Otherwise, there is a possibility that the analysis will take masculine values for granted in technological and social development (Esseveld 1982) and thus serve only to legitimize the present system of sexual hierarchy.

For me, the real strength of a feminist approach to an appropriate TA is in its focus on technology in everyday life and the conflicts and contradictions associated with it. More general theories of technology and society concentrate largely on the productive sphere. I support an approach that includes an analysis of the entire range of work necessary in a society, reproduction as well as production. In other words, assessment of any technology that affects women must look at the tension between these two spheres.

A critical feminist TA is in agreement with Marx's belief that any given social arrangement is historically transient, that it came into being at a particular phase in history and will eventually pass out of existence. Capitalism and patriarchy are not static concepts but alter their character and form as time passes and conditions change. A historical perspective traces technological development in an effort to understand the status quo. It forces the researcher to seek the origins of the technology in question, to ask, where does this come from? who developed it and why? A historical analysis often uncovers interesting and sometimes surprising answers. It can expose the ideological and social power of those who make decisions during the various phases of research, development, and dissemination of technology. As shown in Part III, the reinforcement of old and established forms of power and control are often embedded in the design and organization of technology.

My perspective is optimistic: I see TA as a social process that can be influenced by social forces—consequently, by women. I see TA as an instrument for exercising political and social control over technology. Therefore, I see the possibility that women, by developing a critique of and becoming involved with TA, can make a difference. Their first task is to ensure that they and their roles are made visible. There have been few attempts outside feminist circles to assess the gender-specific impact of technology on women, and very little has been done outside academic circles. A critical TA, at least in theory, opens the door for the inclusion of women as well as the integration of a women's perspective. The involvement of feminist scholars in TA should be encouraged so that they can provide the women's movement with a tool for exercising influence on the course of technology development.

Finally, I see that by being oblivious to, ignoring, or forgetting theory, present methods of TA do not uncover the potential power and control effects of technology. By not including a historical perspective, present methods also fail to reveal the underlying technical, economic, social, and political factors in technological development which can have a detrimental effect for women. If TA does not permit the option of totally rejecting or banning a technology, it limits the opportunity for discussion of alternative solutions.

From the various analyses presented so far in this work, a critical feminist approach to TA emerges. As a human, social, and political activity, TA has been seen as carried out *by* some people and not others; it is also carried out *for* some people and not others. This makes the acknowledgment of various interest groups and their different perceptions of technology and TA an important issue. Social movements, including feminists, have made demands on technological development which can be applied to TA. They advocate a TA that empowers by being based on public participation and by promoting methods of assessment that problematize human needs and contribute to a nonoppressive technological development.

Because technology creates conflicts and tensions within and between various social groups, a TA that seeks to empower (in contrast to supporting the status quo) recognizes that assessment cannot be neutral. An assessment that claims to analyze social consequences must address the fact that technology affects power relations, and the consequences can vary greatly from one group to another. From this perspective, the important issue is not to promote one method or approach of TA over another but to ensure that women and the interests of women are represented in all forms.

Summary

This chapter has argued the importance of a feminist approach, presented and then criticized two attempts to build TA models based on feminist demands, and developed a focused critique of mainstream TA. As a form of summary, I have drawn up preliminary lists of elements which I believe can contribute to a TA that lives up to critical and feminist demands.

I begin with the general approach, which is concerned with the asymmetics of power in society (gender, race, class); views technology as an equity issue; exposes the promotion of technological fixes; is concerned with environmental and cultural conditions; is concerned with sex and gender issues; recognizes the role of economic and political forces in shaping technology; recognizes that TA is not a politically neutral tool; is interdisciplinary; is based on an emancipatory approach; is on guard against theories and methods that can oppress women and other subordinate groups.

A critical feminist TA promotes political consciousness and self-actualization; empowerment and self-help; the option to reject a technology; a search for alternatives; public participation in the TA process; the public's right to information; legislation to control new technology; strategies for social change.

Its methods, with explicit theoretical grounding, make possible an analysis of values; of technological "drift"; of short-term and long-term effects; of gender differences; of technology in everyday life and the conflicts and contradictions associated with it; of technological development in its historical and material context.

The goals of a critical feminist TA are to initiate a process that will contribute to solving a need or problem; to focus on the dynamics of the social process and women's role in or absence from it; to ensure the participation of women as well as a women's perspective.

PART III
Women and Technology: Examples

7
The Clerical Sector

This chapter shows how technological development has affected women in the female-dominated clerical sector, using examples from the introduction of computer technology. The purpose is to demonstrate the importance as well as the difficulties of a gender analysis in TA. Step one is to identify and criticize mainstream TA in the clerical sector; step two, to show through a criticism of studies that do include gender that this is not enough.

The presentation of this material is followed by a critical feminist assessment of women and technology in the clerical sector: I analyze systems of dominance, look at the division of labor by sex, and discuss values, all as they relate to this sector.

Assessment in the Clerical Sector
Existing institutionalized TAs of the clerical sector are usually found within larger studies of the effects of technology on the labor market (ILO 1985a; IMI 1984; OECD 1981). More precise assessments are more difficult to locate. Bevan (1987) reviewed assessments (both institutionalized and non-institutionalized) made during a five-

year period in order to look specifically at the effects of new office technology on secretarial work. He identified three broad approaches, each representing a distinct view of the world and together illustrating the wide diversity of the issues involved.[1]

In the first group, the approach to TA is based on issues of control from a management perspective (Bevan 1985; Colwill 1985; Davin 1984; Duff and Merrier 1984; Hensen 1980; Kendall 1979; Manpower Ltd. 1985; Olsten 1982; Winkler 1985). These studies were designed and structured to look at how technology integrates with office functions. Their methodology can be characterized as a systems-based approach to human-factor issues. From this perspective, TA views secretaries as the core of the clerical sector and as an important part of an office system; regards the secretaries' primary function as processing information through a variety of mechanisms (word processors, communication storage or retrieval); sees technological change as inevitable; considers that the overall objective is to get the work done and meet goals set by the organization; sees a reduction in routine and repetitive tasks as likely; assumes that more variety, responsibility, change, and an expanded role for the secretary will become the norm. The changes that these studies anticipate can best be interpreted as cosmetic adjustments to work content and job descriptions. The conflictual issues that are taken up are predominantly viewed as challenges to managers.

The premise from which studies in the next group approach assessment is that technology exists to absorb programmable tasks, while people are called upon to provide adaptive responses in exceptional circumstances (Bird 1980; Buchanan and Boddy 1982; Fahurich, Fauser, and Heller 1984; Major 1984; Mumford 1983; NEDO 1983; Otway and Peltu 1983; Royal Society of Arts 1981; Silverston and Towler 1984). These studies focus on the man-machine interface and are concerned with how this can be managed to optimize both performance and the quality of working life. They bring to the debate a serious evaluation of the interface between job design and technology, and attempt to define and describe the changes in job content and scope which result from the introduction of new office technology. Their basic premise is that office work is subject to automation. As jobs become irreversibly affected by technology, these studies focus on the quality of working life of those affected and the design of jobs that can help ensure it.

It is characteristic of these first two approaches that although they look at the job of secretary, they do not recognize gender as a factor. In the third, the impact of office technology on secretaries is viewed as a fundamental political, social, economic, and, very often, feminist issue. The assessments in this group range from thorough neo-Marxian writings (Barker and Downing 1980; Breugel 1979; Downing 1980) to historical and sociological discussions (Benet 1973; Delgado 1979; Morgall 1983c; Silverston 1976; SPRU 1982; Vinnicombe 1980). These studies can be characterized as: dealing almost exclusively with the human, political, social, and psychosocial consequences of technology in the workplace; viewing technology as either a threat or a liberator; analyzing more deeply than others the impact of technology on women.

Bevan found no studies that rigorously examined what secretaries want *from* technology that presented either their views or those of trade unions. He summarizes the issues of new technology and the changing role of secretaries as follows:

1 Higher-level junior management tasks are being devalued and assigned to secretaries.
2 There is apparently no replacement of jobs lost by natural attrition.[2]
3 Secretarial work and the position of the secretary are social issues: the secretary's role within a serving and

processing function perpetuates the expectation that she aspires to nothing else and that office technology will serve to reinforce hierarchical power relations.

4 If change is desirable and technology is one major mechanism for initiating change, then practical measures must be adopted to provide secretaries with a truly enhanced role and genuine equality of opportunity.

Problems
Reviewing the studies included in Bevan's categories, I find the approaches of those in the first two groups to be examples that ignore a gender-specific perspective. The first approach, a management perspective, can be criticized because these studies are defined by issues of control: they have a systems-based approach to human factors, and they view change as inevitable. This approach supports a belief in technology as progress, and by introducing strategies for managing it advocates social engineering. Descriptions or predictions of adjustment to the status quo do not seriously question its appropriateness or challenge its legitimacy. By framing the problem in terms of issues of power and control from the managers' perspective only, this approach minimizes any hope of fundamental change for secretaries.

The second approach, assuming that technology absorbs programmable tasks, can be criticized because these studies are concerned with the man-machine interface and how this can be managed. They define changes in job content and scope as the result of technology, taking the technology as given and the effect as inevitable. Like those in the first group, these studies are also clearly expressions of a noncritical approach in that they take for granted that technology is progress. They assume that jobs will be irreversibly affected by the technology, and they do not explore or even consider an opportunity for the job or the person in the job to affect the technology.

All the studies mentioned in these two groups contribute little to a discussion of the position of women or to any process by which secretaries might gain access to decision-making and planning procedures. Their weakness lies in their failure to examine the political, social, and economic position of women. Although they are optimistic and advocate positive change, they lack the understanding of the perceptions of managers and the process of change that is needed to bring the so-called opportunities of technological change to fruition. The studies suffer from a limited understanding of what secretaries themselves aspire to and how this can be achieved. They concentrate on job design but tend to ignore important aspects such as career management and training.

The third group comes closest to a critical feminist approach. These studies belong to the tradition of TA that views technology as social process. Their approach is critical and far less optimistic then the other two about fundamental changes in the role of the secretary through new office technology. These studies address the existing structural and institutional barriers that militate against any change in traditional definitions of social position, economic value, and gender role. They discuss power and control, the position of women at work, the so-called "office wife syndrome,"[3] and the domination by men of meaningful decision-making forums and processes. From this perspective, the impact of technology on women is viewed in the light of other issues, including political and socio-economic matters; sometimes even feminist issues are analyzed in depth. The education system and economic and political structures are examined in detail and cited as major reasons for the lack of substantive progress that feminist writers have predicted and observed.

Bevan criticizes feminist studies for their tendency to argue vigorously for emancipation on behalf of, rather than in conjunction with, a disadvantaged or "oppressed" group—a point with which I agree. It is true that many feminist studies offer no practical suggestions as to how change might be brought about. Although they advocate radical, structural, and societal change, the situation they present and analyze is the status quo, born of the relationship between capital (technology) and labor. These studies view changes in the existing system (at the workplace level) as cosmetic and superficial. Only Barker and Downing (1980) have done a serious analysis of the values and norms of secretarial work, and their study is already dated.[4] Three case studies of TA in the clerical sector, however, do illustrate the diversity of methods and scope in approaches that consider gender.

Three Cases
The following studies regard technology as social process and consider gender as an integral part of TA. My own study Morgall (1983c) appears here as an example of looking at the introduction of new technology from the users' perspective. Two more recent studies are Bevan (1985) and Softley (1985), which look at the effects of new office technology and the job of secretary from the organizational level.

The first case is a long-term study I did in the late 1970s and early 1980s to document the events leading up to the introduction of word-processing equipment in an office. The purpose was to analyze the problems encountered in introducing new technology and its effects in the office. This study was cited in Bevan's review as unique in illustrating technology assessment from the users' perspective. The users were a group of ten secretaries working for a small research institute at the University of Copenhagen. The data, collected through participant observation over a three-year period, included both individual and group interviews. This empirical study in the tradition of action research can be categorized by what Launsoe (1991) calls a "subject perspective," (also called an "actor's perspective").[5]

In 1979, when funds became available for new office and computer equipment, the secretary group decided on their own initiative to survey the market in word-processing equipment. At that time, such equipment was not in widespread use in Denmark, and the group was not aware until later of the potential organizational and occupational health problems.[6] They saw the word processor as an advanced typewriter that could help them with the heavy typing loads estimated to take up 80 percent of their time. Therefore, they formed a purchasing committee whose task it was, first, to evaluate and select the system best suited to the needs of the institute, and then to make a purchase recommendation to the institute board.

They encountered many problems. In the purchasing phase they discovered that sales pitches were of two types, one for secretaries and one for employers: that is, one emphasizing time-saving features and one focusing on potential staff reduction. When the secretaries expressed concern about their work environment and occupational health hazards, they were not taken seriously by sales representatives. For example, "when a secretary made a remark about the screaming green letters on a screen, she was told by the salesman that all you had to do was pull a pair of pantyhose over the screen to avoid eyestrain" (Morgall 1983c, 111).

A different sort of problem arose after the purchase of the first machine. Training was not included in the purchase price, and the instruction manuals had not yet been translated into Danish. Then, once the equipment had been introduced into the workplace, the employers increased the work load, believing that the machines would automatically increase production. With experience, the secretaries' competence did increase, and over the three-year period they purchased several word-processing units.

The impact of this process on the secretaries was multi-faceted. First of all, it increased their awareness about their jobs and their profession. They formed an alliance with female professionals with whom they discussed women's issues. They became more involved in union activities and, in fact, were used by the union as an example for other workplaces to follow. Increased solidarity developed within the group, and a more active role and participation in workplace as well as union activities occurred. Five years later, *all* secretaries had their own word processors; ten years later, members of the entire professional staff had their own units and the number of secretaries had been reduced by half. This outcome was attributed to natural attrition and cuts in the university's budget.

In the second case study, Bevan (1985) looked at the technology then being used by the secretaries in eight organizations, the extent to which the role of secretary within each organization had been altered, and whether the social position of secretaries had been enhanced or stifled by these changes. In order to investigate the impact of office technology on secretarial work, he chose primarily large organizations that had invested heavily in automation and were also known for their work in human resources.

Bevan's main findings were that the secretaries' contact with office technology tended to be almost exclusively with desktop visual display units linked to a mainframe computer. This arrangement permitted word processing, data processing, and electronic mail transfer—but few secretaries actually used the technology to its full potential. The senior secretaries, who tended to be older, often had more problems in accepting and using such equipment, partly because of insecurity and unfamiliarity but partly also because of poor planning and training. The outcome was underutilization of the technology and employee apprehension about its capacity and potential.

In addition, Bevan found that the social position of

secretaries had not changed drastically. "Having" a secretary was still considered by employers a symbol of position, and not being required to share a secretary a true mark of success, upward mobility, and control.

In the third case, Softley (1985) studied eighteen companies in the United Kingdom to discover whether or not word processors had opened new doors for women office workers. She found that no company reported an increase in typists; in fact, of the eighteen, seven companies reported job reductions of about 60 percent. All seven had adopted centralized installations whereby word processors had been introduced into a central typing pool. In the eleven companies in which typing staff had remained constant, seven used fewer than four word processors, and six had substantially increased typists' work loads without hiring extra staff. Moreover, even where the typing staff was not reduced, there was evidence to suggest that many other clerical jobs were lost as a direct result of the introduction of word processing.

Softley found no sign of change in the sex segregation that characterizes the structure of office work in general. Word processors replaced typewriters, but using them remained women's work, while design and maintenance were kept in the male domain. Looking in particular at forms of control, she found that those traditionally derived from male dominance and female subservience had gradually been superseded by more obvious forms such as work measurement.

From the foregoing examination of three case studies we can draw two points to bear in mind. First, an assessment is not necessarily feminist just because it includes gender. Bevan's study (1985) is an example of technology assessment that takes gender into account without being feminist. Although he does look at gender, he does not really analyze it, and his interpretation of secretaries' aspirations and view of their role can be seen as condescending (a problem I consider below in the discussion of values). Second, it may be difficult to find examples of assessment from the perspective of the users in the clerical sector because the women there do not address these issues themselves.

Key Concepts
The question is, what, if anything, can a critical feminist approach contribute to an understanding of the effects of new technology on women in the clerical sector? Are there changes in women's work and status as a result of new technology? The key concepts that a feminist approach to technology assessment must address are systems of domination, the division of labor by sex, and values as they relate to studies in this sector.

Systems of Domination
As a set of social relations with a material base, patriarchy in any branch of the labor market, including the clerical sector, is manifested in the positions women hold and the control exerted over women in the workplace. In the United States, Kanter (1977) found strong patriarchal forces at work protecting and maintaining power in modern office hierarchies, a form of patriarchy that works against women. This can be found in the attitudes and assumptions about women which can be considered reflections of patriarchal relations.

In the approach of the majority of studies criticized here, the most striking observation is the lack of gender as a variable. This is what feminists call making women invisible. Focusing assessments exclusively on the job, the job design, and the technology allows gender to be legitimately ignored. An example is an analysis of the mechanization of the office sector done by Giuliano (1982), who states that "large numbers of women were employed in offices as a direct result of the introduction of the typewriter." This simple explanation neglects the actual labor market and socioeconomic conditions present at the time, not to mention the social status of women. In fact, typewriters had existed for a long time *before* it became attractive to businesses to buy them. The connection between women and typewriters was not so direct. If Giuliano had looked at gender, he would have realized that although the entry of women into the clerical sector occurred during a period of technological change, the reasons were complex, as shown by feminist studies that look beyond the technology itself:

> Feminist research has sought out other variables, such as employment patterns and labor force characteristics, demographics, economic and business conditions, and prevalent ideologies, in order to explain the women-typewriter connections. Thus, the presence of a reasonably well-educated female native-born population, the growth and changing practices of business, the shifting of ideologies in the face of market needs, as well as the new technology itself, are among the complex set of forces contributing to the growth of the female clerical labor force in the United States in the late nineteenth and early twentieth centuries. The typewriter or other office technology no more causes female employment or liberates women than any other single factor could; yet, in combination with other factors, it significantly changed women's lives. [Rothschild 1983, xxiv]

Systems of domination manifest themselves in the very organization of the office. In a recent study of the clerical sector, Webster (1989) found that the degree and type of control exercised by management over the office labor process is mediated by the type of organization and its requirements: its historical use of control strategies, the position of female office workers in the labor market (including the level of wages they can command) within particular industries and geographical areas, as well as the state of the economy in general.

The results of my own study of a secretary group (Morgall 1983c) support these findings. That is no direct or "simple" forms of control were imposed on the group.[7] They had the freedom to choose their own machines and even the chance to reorganize their own work when the machines came (which, unfortunately, they did not do). But outside demands from the university administration and the academic staff placed organizational constraints on the work of the secretaries. Also, the overall social expectations of the job seemed to inhibit any radical change in their function or the structure of their work.

It can be concluded that although this group of female clerical workers had autonomy within their own workplace, they did not have the power and control necessary in the larger societal context to facilitate change. The study illustrates the potential control aspects associated with technological change and the factors that affect the possibility for workplace change as well as for collective action.

Cockburn (1987, 5, 8) reported similar findings in her study of the impact of computerization in eleven different British workplaces:

> When the dust settled after the technological revolution, the same old male/female pattern can be seen to have re-established itself. The general law seems to be: women may press the buttons, but they may not meddle with the works. . . . Always the person who knows best, who has the last say about the technology, is a man. . . .
>
> How has hegemonic masculine ideology dealt with the shift of technology from heavy, dirty and dangerous (electromechanical) technology, to light, clean and safe (electronic) technology, given that masculinity was so clearly associated with the former qualities and femininity with the latter? The ideology has done a neat "about turn." The new technology is associated with logic and intellect and these in turn with men and masculinity. The complement is preserved by associating women and femininity with irrationality and physicality.

Bevan (1987) observed that few secretaries are likely to identify readily with the concept of "patriarchal relations of control." I agree with this, first because the literature supports it, and second because I have seen it in my own research experience. A study done by Burris (1983) had similar results: "Some low-level clerical workers in the U.S. felt extremely positive about word-processing technology, not because of objective improvements in working conditions, but because working with computerized technology gave them a feeling of power and importance. Even the fact that the technology counted their errors was taken as an indication of the importance of what they were doing" (p. 117). Yet what Bevan attributed to low aspirations on the part of the secretaries can be interpreted in many ways. It can be attributed to being kept out of the decision-making process or, as Softley (1985) concluded, to insufficient training.

An extensive interview survey carried out in Finland (Lehto 1989) found that the main problem associated with women's use of information technology is that women have insufficient opportunity to influence the planning of its introduction, and they receive insufficient training in data-processing techniques. The women in the study had received an average of seven days of training in data processing, compared with thirteen days for men.

Bevan found that the secretaries' scope for action was limited by the traditional structure of control in the workplace and the societal expectations for and by the secretaries. We can explore traditional control in the light of the division of labor by sex, but only by analyzing values will we find explanations that remove women from the category of victim of their circumstances.

The Division of Labor
As noted earlier, one contribution of a critical feminist perspective to the field of technology studies has been the further development of the division-of-labor analysis.

Central to this analysis is the role technology plays in maintaining control over women's work and women's lives—especially in the female-dominated clerical sector.

Changes in technology may have different effects at different times, depending on the economy as well as the characteristics of the techniques. Crompton and Reid (1982) have shown that the effect of computerization on clerical work in the 1950s and 1960s was indeed to deskill and thwart opportunities for promotion for clerical staff (women). They point out, however, that the effect of primarily on-line computerization may have the opposite effect.

As already mentioned, my own study showed neither mobility nor change of status for the secretaries as a result of word-processing equipment. This is not surprising, considering the size of the workplace I examined. But even though Bevan's sample was much larger than my own, he too reported that the social position of secretaries had changed very little. Softley, however, in asking whether word processing creates new job opportunities, found the answer to be yes—but not for women. In her view, a breakdown of sex lines downward (not upward)—that is, an increase in the number of male word processors in the United States—indicates the loosening of the traditional association of keyboarding with women. With computer skills being taught in schools to both boys and girls, keyboard work is no longer seen only as women's work. In fact, links between keyboarding and computing are growing stronger, and computing is seen as men's work. There is no sign that sex segregation in the office is softening, however; word processors are replacing typewriters, and women are still doing this work. Their concentration in the clerical sector makes them very vulnerable to office automation. In the United Kingdom women's unemployment, both clerical and general, is rising faster than men's. Present developments point to a future wherein women become isolated in the home, doing remote-based work.

Feldberg and Glenn (1983) found that women have been differentially and more negatively affected than men by changes accompanying office automation. They also found a polarization of job categories and a breakdown of conventional mobility ladders accompanying computerization of the service corporations and "high-tech" firms. It is not surprising that this polarization with regard to occupational status is both paralleling and reinforcing gender segregation.

Other studies report that the effects of new technology on the division of labor, horizontal as well as vertical, have had consequences for women specifically in programming and computer software jobs.

In Finland, where there is very strict vertical and horizontal segregation according to gender, results from an analysis based on empirical data on clerical work (Korvajärvi 1989) show that, despite the great speed of the introduction of new technology, the gendered division of labor seems to remain intact. The study concludes that hierarchical organizational structures are the biggest obstacle to female clerical workers in using new technology to improve their position in the organization.

How is the division of labor affecting the character of the work, and how are women's jobs being affected? In assessing the impact of the word processor on secretarial jobs, Webster (1989) found task fragmentation, deskilling, and work intensification.[8] She attributed these results to the presence and extent of the division of labor rather than to the new technology:

> My studies suggest that the phenomenon of work intensification is, in fact, far more complex than critics of the new technology suggest. The two most crucial determinants of the level of effort exercised by typists are 1) structural, lying in the degree to which the division of labor operates and the consequent extent of confinement of the typist to a single subdivided operation, and 2) normative, relying on managerial pressure on workers to exert themselves. WP

[word-processing] machinery per se plays no significant role in this process." [P. 61].

Women do not have the same job status as men, and there are fewer women in management positions and positions of supervision: for example, 3 percent women versus 14 percent men in Denmark (Ligestillingsraad 1987). Job status and wages were lower for women in the early days of computing (Greenbaum 1976), and this trend continued into the 1980s. Kraft and Dubnoff's (1984) survey found not only that women were concentrated in the lowest-paying software jobs and the worst-paying industries (finance, real estate, and communications) but that they were paid less than men as well.[9]

The detailed division of labor is a requirement of capitalism; the sexual division of labor is a further refinement that fulfills the requirement. In my analysis of the clerical sector, this development is clear. In clerical work as we know it today, a direct outgrowth of capitalist development, women have been the pool of workers serving the classic functions of what Marx described as the reserve army of labor.

Bringing in women to fill newly created positions, or degrading and reorganizing traditional male work and calling it women's work (Morgall 1981c), has kept wages down and discouraged militancy in all workers. In the clerical sector this was done by recruiting middle-class women whose potential for getting jobs was restricted to very few professions, essentially teaching and nursing. From such workers at that time, one would not expect militancy in the job market. These women worked for lower wages, which undermined their collective struggle for a living wage.

Since the 1960s the steady increase in the frequency of women's participation in the labor market, especially the clerical sector, has been widespread in many countries. For example, 54 percent of all French office workers were

women in 1956; the proportion rose to 58.2 percent in
1962. In the United Kingdom, 0.8 percent of office
workers were female in 1851, compared with 59.6 percent
in 1951. Eighty percent of the increase in American white-
collar employees from the mid-1940s to the mid-1960s
was due to the massive recruitment of females (Crozier
1971).

The current status of the vertical division of labor as
it relates to technological development can be found in
Burris's (1989) study of "technocratic organization" as it
relates to gender.[10] In this study, which has tremendous
relevance for the clerical sector, Burris observes what she
calls technocratic control as the latest in a series of
methods for workplace control. In recent years, organizations have been socially and politically transformed
around advanced technological systems, and observable
changes in structure have occurred. "Technocracies" are
characterized by a polarization into expert and non-expert sectors.[11] Burris sees this technocratic reorganization
as paralleling and reinforcing sex segregation, with
women disproportionately found in the "non-expert" sector.[12] The result is that mobility prospects are becoming
minimal or nonexistent, and working conditions are poor.
Even women in the "expert" sector of technocratic organizations are disadvantaged, because persisting stereotypes
define women as antithetical to technocratic norms of scientific rationality.

Today, there is an increase in the geographic division
of labor. This can be found in the increase of remote-
based work in the clerical sector, which affects women
primarily if not exclusively (Vedel 1986).[13] A combination
of computer technology and communication technology
has made it possible for low-level clerical workers to perform their tasks at home on computers. In this way, a
systematic, hierarchical regional division of labor has
been established between different tasks and different
working and living conditions (Morgall and Vedel 1985).[14]

Even in studies of professionals who work at home (e.g., Wajcman and Probert 1988), there is strong evidence of reinforcement rather than transformation of gender differences. For example, an Australian study reports:

> When we asked the programmers and word processor operators in our sample how working from home had changed their attitude to work, we found strong evidence of reinforced rather than transformed gender differences. Whereas the majority of men had become more work-centred, the women were more likely to have become less work-centred and more family-centred. . . . Overall, then, new forms of computer-based homework would appear to reinforce sexual divisions in relation to paid work and unpaid domestic work, as well as to the technical division of labor. Once more we see women failing to gain the genuinely technical jobs, in this case producing software for computers. [Wajcman 1991, 42]

The sexual division of labor in the clerical sector also retains its temporal dimension; it is still characterized by part-time work that puts women at an obvious disadvantage for promotion and the opportunity for more diversified tasks.

In summary, new technology in the office teamed with the reorganization of work appears to be reinforcing the division of labor by sex in general and in the clerical sector in particular, whether horizontal, vertical, geographical, or temporal. Women are disproportionately found in low-level jobs with minimal mobility prospects.

Values

The need to include a gender analysis in technology assessment in order to get at the power and control aspects of technology has been emphasized throughout this work. Although many of the studies on the clerical sector discussed here have included gender, it could be argued that they have contributed little to finding the so-called liberating aspects of technological change for women. Neither of the studies in Bevan's (1987) overview nor the three case studies presented above looked at what the secretary expects of her work or of the technology.[15] I suggest that these studies could have been strengthened with a value analysis.

In my own study I missed an opportunity for a value assessment. I could have analyzed what the job and the future of the job meant to the secretaries. I could have looked at the content and significance of the secretaries' private lives and the relationship between them and their work lives. Bevan (1985), too, missed this opportunity. He could have extended his analysis to ask why the workers *appeared* to have low aspirations at work. Were there other areas of their lives where they had high aspirations?

Softley (1985), though she did not analyze values either, did include a description of how women resorted to sabotage, which I consider a valuable insight into female values. Her study shows that new work-control practices such as monitoring the work load were not passively accepted. Some secretaries sabotaged the work measurement capacity of the machine by finding ways to fool it. Another technique, feigning ignorance about machine malfunctions, gave the secretaries free time while they waited for the technician to arrive. Softley interpreted this as an attempt to regain control at the individual level. It is interesting to note the reaction of the men in the office: machine breakdowns only served to strengthen their belief that women were technologically illiterate. The men did not see a breakdown as involving a conscious action by the women but rather assumed that the women must have done something wrong as a result of a misunderstanding on their part.

Several studies, including Bevan's and my own, report that the potential for secretaries to reorganize their work has been present but not exploited. This was the conclusion of a recent study done in the United Kingdom. Webster (1989) found that although there is potential for redesigning clerical work, limitations include the position of women on the labor market, the current cursory nature of training for office work, and poor levels of unionization among office workers. She attributes to these factors the diminished bargaining position of office workers.[16]

Similar results are reported by Bevan (1985, 188), who also found that opportunities for job redesign when office technology was introduced went unfulfilled: "The expanded role of the secretary, while facilitated by technology, is limited by what [one] might term the 'patriarchal relations of control' which still pertain to the modern office." The conditioning of trainee secretaries to internalize the importance of the secretarial "service" they provide was difficult for them to reject. Bevan reports that many secretaries remain dedicated to the goal of service and judge their success accordingly. As to "feminist consciousness," he concluded that they "would not provide fruitful subjects of consciousness-raising." Their aspiration was very modest, in that they were prepared to accept male domination and the goal of secretarial "service" in return for being treated as "colleagues" rather than commodities signifying their employers' status.

Among those who did object to having few opportunities to realize their potential, and even fewer opportunities to break through the almost impenetrable barrier that separates secretarial from administrative work, many believed that they had "junior management" potential but felt that social rather than technological constraints obstructed their progress. Bevan concludes: "The scope for action by the majority of secretaries is, of course, limited as many work within highly structured and traditional structures of control, as well as within cultures which are less open to change. It would be unrealistic and patronizing to suggest that secretaries should rise up in revolt against oppression in the office" (pp. 189–90).[17]

I see the feminist discussion of values as relevant here.

I believe that the concept of job status and what that costs in nonmonetary terms must be compared with other values and treated as choices, if women are not to be considered helpless victims of the system or simply lacking in ability and ambition. I believe that a value analysis can reveal—from the female clerical workers' perspective—just which values they place on work, their jobs and new technology And, most important, how these values relate to their life as a whole.

One assessment in the clerical sector which does analyze values is Boman's (1981). In a study of the Swedish National Insurance System, she analyzes women's reactions toward the introduction and influence of electronic data processing (EDP) and found that time and time again, women expressed themselves differently from men with regard to the implementation of new technology. Prior to its introduction, the women met in study circles organized by their union for the purpose of discussing and ultimately formulating what they *wanted* from this new development. In assessing the women's arguments and justifications for their demands on the new system, Boman found that unlike traditional union demands such as increases in salary and job redefinition, the women's demands could be seen as expressions of caring and solidarity. In their formulation of demands for the union policy proposal, the women showed concern over what consequences employment and service would have for the social and interpersonal relationships of their clients—parent-child relationships, workplace and intercollegial relations, contact with clients—and whether loneliness and (as a result of unemployment) criminality and other problems would increase.

Boman (1981, 54) attributes the concerns expressed to their basis in female-specific experiences and concludes that "women, from their special experiences and values, have different questions, they present other arguments and express themselves differently from men when discussing computerization" (my translation). These differences in thinking and modes of expression, even in connection with a union policy proposal, were overlooked by the decision-makers, mainly men. In fact, their own male union representatives did not understand the demands and proceeded to reformulate them to resemble more traditional union demands.

I agree with the recommendations of a Finnish analysis of new technology and the division of labor (Korvajärvi 1989), which suggests that the focus of future research should be less on technology and its impacts as such, and more on the gender system and its cultural features in the structures of wage labor.

A last but not least important aspect to consider in a feminist approach is the analysis not only of the values of the women being affected by technology but of the role of experts and the values of mainstream science and technology. What values do the experts bring to technology? What values do the assessors bring to TA?

Summary
This chapter has examined the implications for women of new technology in the clerical sector, criticizing the various approaches and methods of assessment. From examples of the introduction of computer technology, it can be concluded that new technology is being integrated into new and advanced forms of the sexual division of labor. New technology has definitely played a role in cementing and maintaining the complex division of labor by sex. For assessment purposes, the inclusion of gender as a variable is not enough; simply recording women's subordinate position does nothing but reinforce it. A TA that seeks a true understanding of the issues must also take a critical posture toward assumptions of hierarchy, job design, and status.

8

Reproductive Technology

Reproductive technology is one of the fastest growing and most controversial fields of health care technology today. Because the introduction of new reproductive technology is pervasive, and in many cases its effects may be irreversible, it is of major concern to feminist activists as well as scholars. Assessing reproductive technology raises issues of women's autonomy that are of universal interest and applicable to all people and all cultures.

   This chapter looks at the limitations of MTA in light of the development of new human reproductive technology, which—unlike technology in the clerical sector—is almost exclusively for women.¹ The chapter is based on my research in the fields of family planning, abortion, and TA. Its purpose is to make visible the inadequacy of current methods of MTA and, at the same time, to emphasize the complexity of the issues involved.

New Technologies
Reproductive issues of concern to feminists in the 1970s focused on the struggle for access to birth control and abortion: that is, the right *not* to have children. Between

1960 and 1970 more than a dozen new contraceptives reached the market, and there is every expectation that the trend will continue into the future (STG 1987). Given the various new forms of reproductive technology developing today, however, discussions of "reproductive rights" are now focused on the right to have a child (Rose 1987).

The research into reproductive technology is concentrated into two areas: the manipulation of fertility in order to have or not to have children, and "artificial" reproduction combined with genetic engineering. The aim of all forms is to manipulate or interfere with natural functions, either to promote or to prevent having children or to influence the quality of the children born.

Feminist studies have dealt with issues of reproduction as one of their fundamental concerns (Doyal, Kickbusch, and Morgall 1984; Feldman 1987). The ability of each woman to control the number of children she will bear has been regarded as one means of increasing women's influence in the family sphere and female self-determination regarding the frequency (and quality) of sexual relations. Women's control over their reproductive functions has been seen in the broader perspective of having control over their own bodies. The women's health movement was built on these premises.

The development and widespread distribution of oral contraception is often associated with the so-called "sexual revolution" of the 1960s. Although the struggle for women's liberation has been closely associated with liberal access to abortion and family planning, the development of birth control technology is not viewed as unequivocally positive within the feminist movement (Hynes 1989a; Klein 1989; Ratcliff 1989).

I view the history of reproductive technology as a history of the social control of women's fertility.[2] For example, the principle of hormonal contraception was understood in the 1920s.[3] But not until thirty years later was the American nurse and pro-contraceptive activist Margaret Sanger able to "draw the first oral contraceptive preparations from somewhat reluctant scientists and physicians. . . . Although by 1938, the technological prerequisites for the development of an oral hormonal contraceptive existed, prevailing concerns about popular morality and, in some countries, pro-natalist polices delayed this development until the late 1950s" (Newman 1985, 129). The first clinical report of the use of oral steroid hormones to suppress ovulation was published by Gregory Pincus and John Rock in 1956. The approval of the U.S. Food and Drug Administration was granted in 1960, and marketing of the preparations in the United Kingdom began two years later.

The change in public attitudes which legitimized work on "the pill" and at the same time made birth control a respectable issue for public debate was the sudden and popular fear, originating in the United States, of a world population explosion. "Ironically, this fear focused not on the industrialized nations, where both the pressure for reform and the (initial) market for new contraceptive products was greatest, but on the largely agricultural nations of the Third World" (Newman 1985, 130).

When birth control pills are used correctly, less than one woman in a hundred per year experiences an unintended pregnancy. Although controversy concerning contraceptives continues to this day, the medical and technological focus in recent years has been on assisting conception and reproduction rather than trying to prevent them.

MTA: A Feminist Approach

Just as a feminist approach to TA is based on a feminist perspective of technological development, so too is a feminist approach to MTA. Seen in light of the concerns of the women's health movement, medical technology is subject to many of the criticisms aimed at technological development in general. For example, Raymond (1989) takes up issues of male dominance and male values in her critique of what she has termed "Rambo medicine." Rambo medicine is based on heroic male technical prowess that requires high technology, high drama, high publicity, high funding, and high risk for women—with little immediate success but, of course, the promise of it. Such practice is based on extreme optimism, always promising a future that is as yet unrealized.

In addition to the Marxist paradigms of health and medicine (see, e.g., Navarro 1977; Waitzkin and Waterman 1974), the feminist critique of health also adopts a critical perspective on health service organization and the healing professions. More specifically, this critique originated in the women's health movement and incorporates a feminist approach to medicine, including medical practice and services. It regards inequalities in health provision and differences in illness behavior as the products of patriarchy and gender.

Feminist critics have argued that modern medicine makes women into natural patients by regarding them as emotional and complaining (Ehrenreich and English 1973, 1979; Roberts 1981); that modern surgery often inflicts unnecessary procedures on women as patients, such as mastectomy and hysterectomy, even when the benefit of these operations is uncertain (Frankfort 1973; Kasper 1985); that modern obstetrics prevents women from exercising control over the birth of their children (Oakley 1980; Starr 1982); that medicine in general prevents women from having control over their bodies, especially with respect to reproduction (Yanoshik and Norsigian 1989); and that "medicalization" turns normal body functions (menstruation, pregnancy, childbirth, menopause) into medical problems (Ehrenreich and English 1973; Reissman 1983).

Critical perspectives in contemporary medical sociology argue that the health of human populations is a consequence not of medical intervention but of the sociopolitical environment. This critique (shared by feminists) is aimed at the modern health care system, which is characterized by a sharp division of labor (based on social group status and sex), increasing specialization, and capital-intensive centralization of services and technology (Waitzkin 1978). The modern health care system is analyzed as a history of professionalism, elitism, and specialization. This increasingly specific division of labor, together with the rapid development and dissemination of new and sophisticated medical technologies, has supported the specialization of medical care, with new specialties which are built up around advanced and constantly evolving diagnostic and therapeutic technology (Buch Andreasen 1988).

The "Medical Model" Approach
Feminist studies have criticized not only the services and organization of the health care sector but also both the theoretical basis of modern medicine—the "medical model"—and the most dominant method of TA, the controlled clinical trial (CCT). Much of this criticism originated in the field of medical sociology and has been elaborated by feminist scholars. An insight into the theory and the method provide a framework for understanding the feminist criticism of medical technology and institutionalized MTA.

As the basic paradigm of medicine, the medical model conceptualizes the human body as a machine (Capra 1986).[4] Since the development of the germ theory of disease in the nineteenth century, it has formed the knowledge base of scientific medicine. Its fundamental assumptions are that disease is caused by the presence of germs and viruses; that the body is a machine which, when ill, is in need of repair (therefore, the patient becomes a passive target of medical intervention); and that treatment is based on the negation of the invading germs or viruses or bacteria.[5] The medical model provides the framework for

understanding, explaining, diagnosing, and treating illness. It is a biophysical reductionist model of illness
which is widespread and dominant in medical practices.
It is an ideology that justifies the use of medical technology, thereby precluding alternative therapies and procedures.

Most MTA is based on the medical model, but its limitations for assessment are manifold. First, the belief that
medical technology can eliminate disease assumes that
the cause of all disease is biological. Second, the assumption that the body can be repaired and illness cured with
the help of modern technology ignores "natural" and alternative methods of treatment and confuses treatment
with cure. Third, the element of social control—that patients have little say in their treatment: doctor knows
best—puts the patient in the position of a passive partner
who must follow the doctor's orders if he or she wants to
be healthy. I would argue that therapy (as well as MTA) is
more likely to be effective when the patient is regarded as
a person with social and psychological needs.

The extensive reliance on controlled clinical trials is a
serious hindrance to assessment.[6] For example, even
though CCTs were done on birth control pills, DES, and
thalidomide before they were marketed, this method did
not reveal their serious long-term side effects. I consider
the fact that CCTs seldom address policy issues as a major drawback. Although TA is by definition broadly based
(that is, multidiciplinary), whereas the focus of CCTs is
extremely narrow, they continue to be the most frequently used single method in MTA. To prove this point,
Brook (1986) did a literature review of all clinical trials
performed in an ambulatory setting during a five-year period. He found that only three of seventy studies looked at
anything except physiological outcome. The three exceptions distinguished themselves by being multidisciplinary
in their outcome measures: they used both cost estimates

and psychological effects. Unfortunately, even when CCTs *are* done in conjunction with other methods, those other methods are most likely to be economic; very little assessment includes human, psychological, and social variables, and I have never seen gender or other relevant social variables taken up in the mainstream literature.

Medicine and Power

In addition to the critique of the medical model as the basic paradigm of MTA, and CCTs as the dominant method, the feminist critic of medicine must confront another major issue: asymmetries of power with regard to class and gender. The research involved addresses the following five aspects:

1 Restricted access to medical technology and services. It is most often the medical profession[7] that decides who qualifies for a given treatment.[8]
2 Medicalization of the female body. This includes defining both normal bodily functions (menstruation, pregnancy, childbearing, and menopause) and social issues (rape, violence) as medical problems requiring medical solutions. The medicalization of birth has turned normal pregnancies into medical events. Medical interference that attempts to control the birth process includes IVF, chemical and surgical means of inducing birth, routine cesarean sections, ultrasound scanning, and amniocentesis, to name but a few.
3 A male-dominated medical hierarchy. The male minority (physicians) are in the decision-making positions; women, who make up the majority of health workers (nurses, nurses aides, home visitors), are in the lower ranks with little decision-making power. Moreover, deskilling of traditional female health professionals (nurses and midwives) has resulted from

the adoption of new medical technology such as that used in monitoring and controlling birth.

4 Medical authority. Within the past hundred years the medical profession has gained much prestige, power, and therefore authority, an authority often compared to that which the clergy previously enjoyed in Western culture. Historically as well as today, the field of medicine is one of the most important ideological forces in society because it defines what "a normal woman" is.

5 The status of women as providers of health care. This includes the "invisibility" of women as traditional providers of "unpaid" care, as well as the working conditions and occupational health issues of "paid" female health workers.

All these issues have implications for TA. Any study of the health care sector involves issues of gender as well as sex.

A basic problem tackled by feminist researchers is the attempt to untangle the confusion between sex and gender: that is, to make visible the gender aspects of women and health. This has been important in arguing against biological determinants as the only important factor in studying women and health. For example, in the nineteenth century, various medical theories suggested that the female personality was determined by anatomy and reproductive function. Gynecology became absorbed in the combat between the brain and the uterus for domination over the female persona (Ehrenreich and English 1979). In the late 1800s, studies equating brain size with intelligence offered as "proof" of woman's inferiority the face that her brain, as well as the rest of her body, was smaller on average than that of a man. George Romanes, author of *Mental Evolution in Man* (1889), based his views of the mental difference between the sexes on the "missing five ounces of the female brain": the fact that the average brain weight of women is about five ounces less than that of men. He concluded that women's brains must therefore be inferior in intellectual power. It was feminist studies that challenged such absurd theories.

Although a feminist approach to MTA differs very little from a feminist approach to TA in general, there are some important differences, which are clarified by the following case. The harmful side effects of birth control pills range from weight gain and emotional mood swings to the more serious increased risk of blood clots. Immediate adverse side effects include nausea, breast tenderness, and headaches. It was only after the first few million women had used the method for several years that patterns of longer-term side effects were reported, such as blood clots that can cause strokes. Despite the use of birth control pills by some fifty million women, little research into the detrimental effects over time has actually been done (Petersen 1984).

More advanced, technically sophisticated technologies involve genetic manipulation of human germ cells and fertilized eggs, as well as powerful hormones. These methods have potentially serious side effects, which may take more than one human generation to manifest, possibly causing irreversible effects on future generations. Consider the case of DES, a synthetic female hormone administered to pregnant women in the 1950s. Although CCTs showed DES to be *ineffective*, the promotion by industry continued. In the United States alone, an estimated 100,000 women took the drug during pregnancy. Almost twenty years later the long-term effects began to surface, and DES was linked with damage to millions of the children born to the women who had taken it (Dierecks 1986), including a rare form of vaginal cancer in the girls.

Problems debated today in connection with reproductive technology are as numerous as they are complex (see Koch and Morgall 1987). There are *ethical and legal questions* that include, for example, when does an embryo become a person? Who owns and controls an embryo in human experimentation? Who owns and controls an embryo produced in a glass dish? If an embryo is frozen and the parents die, what is to be done with it?

Among *social implications*, one well-founded fear is that normal fertilization might be replaced by in vitro fertilization (IVF) and gene therapy, since potentially, genetic disease could be entirely prevented by combining these procedures.

In determining *social roles*, what are the criteria for parenthood, and who decides what or who is a parent: the woman who bears the child? the woman who donates the child? the women who donate ova? the natural father? the men who donate sperm?

Finally, there are *economic issues*: the tremendous cost of these technologies to public as well as private entities; the potential for the commercialization of sperm, ova, embryos, and babies.

MTA from a Feminist Perspective

Together with Lene Koch, I attempted a feminist-oriented assessment of reproductive technology (Koch and Morgall 1987).[9] The purpose was twofold: to elucidate the gender implications in a field closely linked to biologically determined phenomena, and to perform a critical review of existing methods of assessment in a search for those that could provide understanding of the complex issues of women and reproduction.

In an attempt to determine the needs of a feminist approach to TA, we used the case of IVF in Denmark. We found it problematic, from a woman's perspective, that this technology had never undergone formal assessment prior to its application. It was even more surprising—and unusual internationally—that IVF had so quickly become listed as the standard treatment for involuntarily infertile women.[10] The reason is simply that there is no tradition for assessing new medical technology prior to clinical application.[11] We found this strange, in light of the fact that in the Nordic countries there is a centuries-old tradition for the special control of drugs, and that drugs are subject to very strict legislation not only in Denmark but in most of the Western world.

We felt that IVF should have been and should be assessed for several reasons: the treatment is expensive for the national health system (the standard three-cycle treatment costs the equivalent of $12,000); the success rate is low (the take-home baby rate is less than 20 percent); there are unknown risks to both the woman and the child; and the technology is exclusively for women.

The study of IVF from a feminist perspective can be approached in many ways. One issue has been the restricted access to medical technology and services. It is most often the medical profession that decides who qualifies for IVF treatment, yet the selection of eligible women is based not solely on medical criteria but also on exclusion criteria that include civil as well as economic status. Single and lesbian women with precisely the same physiological problems as married or cohabiting heterosexual women are excluded from treatment in Denmark by a political decision. In support of this view, authorities argue that a stable heterosexual family constitutes the optimal home situation for a child. It is difficult not to consider such practices discriminatory, and the attitude shows clearly that the technology of IVF exists in a social structure and organization that are not directed toward the needs of all infertile women. The criteria for inclusion in the program make it clear that IVF is not only a treatment for infertility but also a means of social control.

In our assessment, we distinguished between IVF as a means of curing infertility and IVF as a precondition for a variety of research procedures with different purposes. Considering the far-reaching implications of IVF, we asked ourselves exactly what it was we were dealing with.[12]

Was this an ethics debate or an assessment of reproductive technology? We found evidence that, in fact, the ethical debate had taken over the role of an assessment process. We reviewed the literature and identified the concerns of the lay public with regard to IVF: Should manipulation of the genetic makeup of the fertilized egg be allowed? Who should decide what diseases, if detected in a fetus, warrant an abortion? Do we have the right to interfere with the results of millions of years of evolution?

We found that the American Ethics Committee had expressed concern that obtaining eggs expressly for basic research on pre-embryos should not put the donor (the woman) at any significant risk. We felt that the increased demand for embryos and ova would result in increased pressure on women to donate eggs, even if clinical reasons weren't justified. We also pointed out that women, regardless of the detriment to their bodies, might be pressured to donate embryos or eggs in the name of science.

Putting the focus on the embryo makes the risks to women secondary and side effects tolerable.[13] All research on embryos requires access to the female egg through the female body. Therefore, the entity to be debated must be the woman, her body, her person. The aspiration of eggs from a woman for the single purpose of obtaining eggs cannot be considered risk-free.[14]

We found that a major problem in doing MTA on in vitro fertilization is to distinguish between an assessment that regards IVF as a means of curing fertility and one that sees it as a precondition for a variety of research procedures with different purposes. From a feminist perspective, the important point is to put women in focus, not the technology. Although an MTA that begins with the technology will most likely show us future options, we were reminded of Bush (1983), who says that every technology has a valence, and the valence of IVF seems to be control: control of reproduction, control over which women should bear children, and what type of children they should bear. The question is, *who* should have this control?

Of the existing and most frequently used methods of TA as reviewed in Chapter 3, it is difficult to see which, if any, would benefit assessment of reproductive technology in general and of IVF in particular. Perhaps with the exception of future workshops, the possibility of totally rejecting the technology in question is not really an option in most methods, which do not challenge the technology but rather take it as given. For example, it would be not only unethical but cruel to carry out CCTs as a double-blind experiment in IVF, allowing women in the placebo group to believe that they were being treated when in fact they were not. CCTs would also be inadequate in that they are normally restricted to physiological variables. Of the synthesis methods, literature reviews and meta-analysis may be premature and, as the literature is primarily based on CCTs, would give only a clinical evaluation at best. Nor do they take women's social and psychological needs into consideration. Risk assessment as well as the group process methods could be useful *if* they took women's psychological and social needs into account and if they addressed, the real issues: infertility and genetic screening, rather than the IVF technique itself. A major problem with these methods, however, is selecting the people to represent the public. To whom should this job be entrusted?

We determined that a woman-specific assessment of new reproductive technology is a necessity, and after reviewing the limitations of various methods we decided that there are definite advantages to a need-oriented approach. We found it vital for ethical issues to include sex-related differences and criteria.

We concluded that there are four reasons to pursue a feminist approach to assessment of reproductive technology: women's bodies are the immediate objects of intervention; the introduction and expansion of new reproductive technology will change the social relations between the sexes in a direction that may be detrimental to women's position in society and the family; new reproductive technologies can fundamentally change the concepts of maternity and paternity, as well as the social and cultural structures surrounding women's lives and bodies; and new reproductive technologies are the key to the age of genetic engineering of the human body and the human race. On all these grounds, an assessment including women's social and cultural experiences is vital for future decisions in this area.

Key Concepts

As I did for technology in the clerical sector, I want to address the three key concepts of a feminist approach to MTA. Unlike the clerical sector, reproductive technology does not offer examples of institutionalized MTA in a form suitable for sociological analysis. There are several reasons for this. One is that because MTA established itself independently only in the last half of the 1980s, published materials include little more than overviews of issues and plans, as well as questions posed for public debate (e.g., *Fremskridtets Pris* 1984). Another reason is that most MTA literature in this field is clinical in approach; lacking psychosocial variables, it does not lend itself to scrutiny of the requirements for a broad-based assessment. This discussion is therefore limited to specific references, as it is the entire approach to MTA that I question.

Systems of Domination

In the field of MTA, the lack of gender analysis makes patriarchal relations immediately visible. Focusing assessment exclusively on physical variables is one example of how gender can legitimately be ignored. But lack of gender is not the only variable with psychosocial implications which is regularly ignored. MTA depends almost exclusively on CCTs and economic analyses (that is, those regarding costs, not economics, as a factor in women's lives); even standard social variables such as occupation are often lacking. For example, a systematic omission in the numerous studies of premature delivery has been the nature of women's employment (Messing 1983), yet occupation could explain such causes as stress, exposure to dangerous and toxic substances, the effects of shift work, and so on.

In general, one can debate whether women *want* or *ask for* various forms of technology, but it is no exaggeration to say that women have actively supported attempts to develop better and more effective contraception technology. And there is no denying that today, especially among infertile women, there is a big demand for new reproductive methods. In the United States an estimated one million infertile women have sought help.[15] The focus on new methods has led to controversies among feminist activists and academics over whether the developments are good for women.[16] The question is whether new reproductive technology is increasing women's autonomy or creating the ultimate oppression: that is, taking reproduction out of the hands of women altogether and forever. In my own research on family planning services (David et al. 1990) and abortion (Osler, Morgall, and Jensen 1990), I interviewed over a hundred women about sex, contraception, and fertility. It was rare to find a woman who was aware of the rapid and far-reaching developments in reproductive technology, and even more rare to find one who had a considered opinion on these matters. The challenge to a feminist approach to TA is to develop methods for identifying women's concerns.

A historical overview of reproductive technology clearly shows the presence of patriarchal relations in the form of regulation and control of women. This has been achieved both by limiting access to contraceptive methods and by making them available. From such a long history of reproductive technology, it can be concluded that public policy has not always been supportive of women's desire to regulate their fertility. So powerful and restricting have public opinion and policy been that contraceptive methods have at times been held back and made illegal. For example, much written obstetrical and gynecological knowledge was destroyed as a result of witch burning in the seventeenth century. Abortion was illegal in most countries until well into the twentieth century, and its legality is still being hotly debated in many parts of the world.

There is a marked difference between methods known and methods available and used. I agree with Elverdam (1984), who maintains that the desired rate of childbirth is determined by a society's material means of production, which in turn affects the choice among various means of birth control and abortion and the frequency with which they are utilized.[17] In the anthropological literature, descriptions of methods of abortion occur more frequently than those for birth control (Elverdam 1984). It appears that abortion is one means of preserving autonomy in societies that narrowly restrict mothers or punish untimely pregnancies. Yet abortion has carried the highest penalties, including death, forced labor, and imprisonment.

Critical feminists see the future of reproductive technology as threatening the control women have over their own fertility. Oakley (1987) argues that the medical "management" of pregnancy and childbirth by a powerful male elite has reduced women to the status of reproductive objects and engendered adverse emotional experiences for childbearing women.

Perhaps the most dramatic (and macabre) example of medical control over women's bodies in modern times is postmortem maternal ventilation (PMV), a relatively low-tech procedure used to sustain pregnancy in brain-dead women.[18] Though little mentioned, PMV has been used in the United States and parts of Western Europe for some fifteen years. The assessment of this procedure is an example of the predominant focus on fetal rights in the ethics debate today: standard, frequently used methods such as cost-effectiveness analysis were applied, with the result that PMV was found to be cost-effective because it requires only standard hospital life-support equipment and decreases the need for high-cost prenatal technology (Murphy 1989). The procedure is therefore seen as the means of obtaining the goal (a life saved) at the lowest possible cost. A cost-effectiveness analysis does not question the ethics of making this procedure available or provide any criteria for its use.

Among the questions addressed by a feminist approach to MTA are these: Are new reproductive technologies a tool for women's liberation or a means of controlling them? Does a given procedure threaten women's dignity? Will the so-called freedom from childbearing, as promised by new technology, actually become a form of female bondage which offers men, and the medical profession, an unprecedented opportunity to assert control over the one aspect of the life process which has eluded them until now—human reproduction?

Another area of dominance being analyzed by feminists is technological change as it develops and restricts access to medical technology and services. This is especially true of new reproductive technologies that require a third party, sometimes a donor, and always medical specialists.

There is also the "technological imperative" to contend with in reproductive medicine.[19] Oakley (1987, 46) finds this to be intrinsic to the defense of doctors' claims of professionalism: "Indeed, retention of absolute control over technical procedures is clearly an absolute necessity for the survival of modern medical power." She argues that technology is particularly attractive to obstetricians because technology such as the stethoscope and fetal monitoring enable male doctors to claim to know more about women's bodies than the women themselves know.

Kirejczyk (1990) points out the problem of the coercive nature of medical technology. Medical practitioners, who regard the availability of new reproductive technology as imperative, promote these procedures by drawing the patients' attention to them. The patients in turn fear that they may later regret not using all available means and therefore enter into the treatment protocol.

Division of Labor
The division-of-labor analysis of technological development and its effect on women is more direct in carrying out TA in the labor market. Seen in its broadest sense, however, this analysis has relevance also in understanding reproductive technology both historically and in today's health care sector. According to Ehrenreich and English (1979), the fear some feminists express about the increasing control of women's bodies by the medical profession is not unfounded. They point out that in the history of the medical profession there is a long record of men's usurping control of medical technologies, to their own advantage.

The history of modern medicine from a feminist perspective is a story of the systematic undermining of traditional women healers—their knowledge and practice—which began on a large scale with the witch burnings of the seventeenth century. In step with the rise of the medical profession, midwifery has been all but eliminated in many countries. In the United States it was formerly banned by law and has only recently resurfaced, albeit under strict legislation. The European trend is for midwifery to become a specialty within the nursing profession and no longer an independent profession. An increase in medical interference has followed the medical profession's attempt to enlist the help of new technology in controlling the birth process. Feminists call this the process of medicalization and technification of women's bodies. The result is that almost all births now take place in hospitals under the authority of the doctor, with midwives (if any) assisting. If both doctor and nurse are working on shifts, those professionals who were present at the beginning of labor will not necessarily be present for the birth. From a woman's perspective, this change has affected the continuity and quality of care.

Technology's role in this process increases as new and more sophisticated innovations are introduced: chemical and surgical means of inducing birth, ultrasound scanning and amniocentesis (which are increasingly becoming routine procedure),[20] and IVF, to name but a few. All of these have come under the control and authority of medical doctors and led to a systematic deskilling of traditional female health professions such as nursing and midwifery. The introduction of new technology has also negatively affected women's job placement in the medical hierarchy.

Given the need for secrecy during certain periods of history, it has been difficult to investigate women's access to and satisfaction with various contraceptive methods. Christmas-Moeller (1984) hypothesizes that in order for contraceptive practices to have survived various forms of suppression, a female subculture where knowledge is handed down orally must have existed. This appears to be the only feasible explanation, since no written records survive. It is her hypothesis that the primary carriers of such a subculture were healers, prostitutes, and midwives.[21] She hypothesizes that forbidden information was handed down during the period midwives spent with women before, during, and after the delivery of their children. Another possible source of information is the female network. A Danish tradition from 1500 until the late 1800s was to hold parties two weeks after a birth, attended only by women. These parties gave women the opportunity to exchange information that was not officially allowed, especially during periods of religious and political suppression.

Industrialization and urbanization can perhaps explain why, at the end of the 1800s, numerous preparations were marketed for contraceptive use, most of which had no effect at all. This has been interpreted as a sign that there was a breakdown not only in the role of midwives but also in the informal female structure that had preserved traditional practices (Christmas-Moeller 1984). I view the current situation and feminist debate concerning women's alienation from the development and use of new reproductive technologies as related in part to this breakdown in the informal female network and the undermining of the role of the midwife at the time of increasing male dominance in the birthing process. In response to what feminists considered biased and often demeaning services, the women's health movement set up alternative services in the 1980s. These services, often clinics staffed by professional female volunteers, were designed to meet the physical, psychological, and social needs of women.

Access to safe contraception and abortion has been (and still is) strongly influenced by religious and political interests and, increasingly in the past century, the medical sector as well. These are three areas where women traditionally have had very little power and authority, especially professionally.

Values
The development of new reproductive technology is accelerating at tremendous speed, and the issues affecting the future role of women in reproduction are extremely complex, as exemplified by the case of IVF. The very complexity of these issues creates a challenge for TA, especially for a feminist approach. This field of technological devel-

opment, more than others, would benefit from an analysis of values.

In addressing the question of values, the analyses of Walden (1982) and Gilligan (1982) are most relevant. In the study of IVF, we found the alternative to a fetus-oriented ethics debate to be a discussion of values (Koch and Morgall 1987). Gilligan's formula of rights, ethics, equity, non-intervention, and self-assertion must be completed by the ethics of responsibility and its respect for differences, human relations, and understanding.

If one agrees that individuality and self-assertion are qualities that many women have found it difficult to develop, and that devotion and self-sacrifice in the interest of others[22] are more often pronounced in women's identity, then we see how women can easily be losers if fetus-oriented ethics remain the basis of reproductive decisions. In our IVF case, we found that the bulk of existing ethical writing is fetus-oriented rather than woman-oriented. We recommended the necessity of an ethical debate to supplement TA in the field of reproductive technology. The weakness in our work was that we offered no suggestions for an appropriate methodology to explore these far-reaching, complicated, and conflict-filled issues. Reliable methods are especially needed when the issue is as emotionally charged as IVF.

Spallone (1987), discussing the implications of feminist ethics in issues of reproductive technology, recommends that health care and medical research be neither embryo-centered nor progress-centered but woman-centered. She suggests that the aims of reproductive health care and medical research should be focused on what serves women best, not what serves scientists best.

Another aspect of a value analysis that is highly relevant for reproductive technology, the social construction of infertility (Koch 1989), is based on the prevalent idea that a female is not a woman until she becomes a mother. In a Norwegian study of infertility, Leira (1987) attempted to analyze the ways women dealt with the crisis of finding out they could not have children. She concluded that women's desire to have children was a result of their socialization and a formulation of the female identity that prepared them from birth to fulfill the role of mother.

In conclusion, it can be said that any approach to MTA that perceives the human body as a machine (such as the medical model) and any method that concentrates solely on physiological variables (such as CCTs) cannot live up to feminist scrutiny.

Summary

Reproductive technology is one of the fastest growing and most controversial areas of health care technology today and well illustrates the complexity of the issues. Sophisticated new methods and procedures threaten women's social and biological role in reproduction. As a result, conflicts and tensions have arisen in society and among women. The relationship between technology and the future of motherhood has created a situation of extreme ambivalence for women today.

This chapter has pointed out the inadequacy of present forms of MTA in getting at the real issues that are important to women. I have found the major problems to be results of the lack of an explicit theoretical and methodological approach; the inadequacy of implicit theoretical grounding based on the medical model in capturing and analyzing nontechnical, nonphysiological issues; the absence of the option to reject new reproductive technology; the need for an ethical debate; and the need for empirical data that deal with women's needs and desires for future reproductive technology.

There is no final and absolute conclusion. The issues are too complex and too new, and the implications of these developments for future generations is virtually unknown.

Conclusion
Drawing Out Criteria for a Critical Feminist Approach

My analysis leads me to conclude that the major reason TA has done little to serve women's interests is that the questions specific to women's lives are never asked. My proposal is a new approach, based on a belief that technological development is a social process that interacts with other social processes. Although I am unable to offer an alternative to present methods, I have developed overall criteria for what I call a critical feminist approach to TA. I propose that to understand and predict the effects of technology on women, TA must address the realities of everyday life, including gender. This means that in addition to a broad assessment of the technological development itself, TA should address other social relations such as domination, the division of labor by sex, and values.

My criteria for this approach appear schematically in Table 4 and are elaborated in the remainder of this chapter.

Theoretical Considerations
A critical feminist approach to TA should be interdisciplinary, rejecting any one method or any simple cause-and-effect approach. It should be open to the theories and

Table 4
Summary of a Critical Feminist Approach
to Technology Assessment

Overall Approach

- interdisciplinary rather than monodisciplinary
- theoretically grounded
- contextual rather than fragmented
- dialectic rather than simple cause-and-effect
- addressing knowledge and organizational interests
- addressing systems of domination, the division of labor by sex, and values
- exploring alternatives
- democratic

Questions

Origins: Where does this technology come from?

Use: What was the original intended use?

Relevance for women: How does this technology affect women's status (social, economic, health, etc.)?

Potential for change: Are there opportunities for change due to this technology? Is it potentially liberating or potentially controlling? What are the helping/hindering factors?

Potential for action: What are the opportunities for individual/collective action?

Conflicts & tensions: What conflicts and tensions does this technology raise?

Interests: Who is interested in promoting this technology? Why now? What economic interests does it serve?

Need analysis: Does this technology solve or create a problem for women?

Methods

Trend analysis: identification of similar trends in society

Temporal dimension: historic and future perspective

---

methods appropriate for the specific technology; that is, assessment of technology used for work requires a labor market analysis, whereas an assessment of breast cancer treatment must analyze the patient's rights. It is essential that empirical work not be a substitute for theoretical

analysis. As demonstrated, most methods can be traced
back to implicit theoretical roots. By making explicit the
theoretical framework, one avoids the problems of confusing method with procedures and of using methods that
are totally atheoretical, methods whose definite theoretical moorings are unknown to the assessors, or methods
based on theories that are not capable of assessing technology in the context of everyday life.

It is also important that theories dealing with aspects
of technology and social reality have an economic compo-
nent. Although theories of women and technology should
not be reduced to economic causes, it must be recognized
that gender relations have their roots in actual social relations and that in our society social relations include
economic reality. To propose one general criterion would
be impossible; it would always be dependent upon an ex-
act repetition of events, and that can never happen. This
is one reason why CCTs cannot be a substitute for an
analysis of social factors. A critical approach implicitly
rejects methods that restrict themselves to investigating
observable particulars and thereby close off central aspects of social reality.

It is essential to assess technology within an actual
social context: that is, to look at specific forms of technology aimed at specific groups in specific settings at specific times in history. The theoretical framework must
allow for a variety of social variables, rejecting one-dimensional models, and be dialectic in its approach. A
goal of the assessment must be to make visible the contradictions and the variety of interests in technological development, and to see these in the light of a more advanced synthesis. In studies of women and technology,
this means recognizing the conflict and contradictions in
women's lives.

In building on the feminist contribution, analyses of
systems of domination, division of labor by sex, and
values should be addressed. The results are often surpris-

ing, revealing not only the social constraints on women's lives but also how women react, adapt, or rebel, as the case may be. These analyses have relevance for other subordinate groups as well.

I propose an approach to TA and MTA that is both critical and feminist, a tradition of thinking more than a prescribed method. It emphasizes the necessity of being interdisciplinary: a critical feminist approach seeks to reintegrate disciplines. The division of labor in the humanities and social sciences and the natural and technical sciences has become very advanced, and in order to be effective, TA needs input from several areas.

The overall approach must allow for an exploration of alternatives to the technology being assessed. The technology must not be seen as the only solution to the problem it seeks to solve. This is what gives a feminist approach its emancipatory potential. To examine the alternatives is to see technology as a process of social choices. It opens the possibility to say no to new technology or to restrict future use of established technology.

A democratic approach to TA acknowledges confidence in public participation by political movements and public interest groups. It assumes that solutions to problems caused by technology require a redistribution of political power as much as the insight of technical expertise (Dickson 1984).

Research Questions

In order to explore the knowledge and organizational aspects of technology, a critical TA must first address the question, who developed this technology (the military, industry, private or public research and development)? The next question is, what was the original intended purpose (warfare, industrial use, animal husbandry, consumer product)? Technology is the result of a long research and development process. That process, in turn, is the result of a long-standing desire to extend human abilities. It is relevant to ask, what human or mechanical function does this technology aid or replace? Which social organizations and social relations will it affect?

Because changes in technology are always precipitated or followed by social change in one way or another, it is important to ask, what systematic procedures or modes of work will accompany and follow the use of this technology? A feminist approach asks, what does this technology mean for women? Will it be used exclusively by women (reproductive technology), or is it intended for use by a group that is predominantly women (office technology)? What are the potentially liberating or controlling consequences of this development? What factors help or hinder this potential?

These same questions should be asked with regard to the options for individual and collective action, making the interests of involved parties visible by distinguishing between specific and general interests. It is also important to analyze the tensions and conflicts of interest, either real or potential, between various parties. Such tensions are the culmination of social, ideological, economic, and human interests. For example, in the case of reproductive technology, capital-intensive technological care is accorded high status and commands a large portion of resources in developed countries; consequently, reproductive technology is a prime area for professional career development.

Women often find their ideas and desires in conflict with their role expectations (internal as well as external). As tension increases, they seek to resolve it by changing what they are doing, moving from one position to another, or abandoning one set of ideas in favor of another. Women are not totally free to make these choices, being limited in their action and reactions by their culture, their social position, their sex, and perhaps also by their age, race, and life experience. None of these circumstances, however, can be totally determinant because they suggest conflicting meanings. Current policy comes to the individual from the state, the workplace, unions, the health care sector, and other individuals. Important issues vie for women's attention and invite a following. Then, as circumstances change, as new technologies become available, new decisions are required.

Identifying these conflicts and contradictions must be a goal of research. For example, the major weakness of consensus methods of TA is that a consensus view will not be the outcome of an assessment of all the facts, because facts are not neutral in the face of conflicting interests.

Whether one must choose between a career and part-time work, or between accepting infertility and receiving IVF treatment, these choices exist between what is best for the individual woman and, in a larger context, what is best for women in general. These two issues may be in conflict. If a woman chooses part-time work, she will have less stress and more time to develop other aspects of her life (even to meet the demands of a double work load). This choice may benefit the individual woman in her immediate situation. If all women in the same situation react in the same way, however, a weakening of women's position in the labor market in general will follow, resulting in negative economic consequences and limited possibilities for professional advancement. Likewise, infertility rates continue to rise, yet solutions seem to be technological: new, sophisticated, expensive medical and drug treatments. A woman approaching thirty-five years of age who discovers she has problems conceiving may see IVF as her last chance to have children, and the treatment may solve this particular woman's problem. Yet over time it can weaken women's position in general, since the causes of infertility (environmental influences, social pressures, poor nutrition, pollution, stress) will never be seriously considered as long as the society creating the infertility is prescribing the treatment.

These are the real conflicts and contradictions. Individual women do what they can to redress the inequalities they face. Who can blame them? Women's interests and needs cannot be analyzed as stagnant concepts. But a critical approach focuses on the real needs of many real people; otherwise we may never ask, are there any alternatives to this technology which are better or just as good at solving the problem? And, perhaps just as important, do we have any chance of directing the social and research development in the direction of our needs? If TA is to be used as an instrument for research policy in society, the basis must be an outline of the needs of that society.

Methods

Methods are born of theory, which in turn is intimately related to the research questions. No one method can produce definite results. An interdisciplinary approach makes it possible to use both qualitative and quantitative methods, which can supplement each other in systematic investigations and shed light on needed areas of empirical research.

Proactive, need-oriented TA and MTA have the potential to predict and prevent unwanted effects for women. Much can be learned from retroactive studies, however, especially in the area of reproductive technology. A historical analysis is an asset not only for retroactive but for proactive studies, as well as trend analysis. Current methods using future-oriented (predictive) research—the scenario approach, trend analysis, the Delphi Technique, future workshops—cannot be done in a historical vacuum. Just as has been suggested for CCTs, these methods should be built into larger, theoretically based projects, not stand alone as TA.

There is also a need for a temporal dimension as well as trend analysis in TA, especially for medical technology. History has shown, through the DES example and the thalidomide scandal, that some technologies—especially those with the potential to alter genetic material—have side effects that first become visible only in the next generation. This is also true of occupational health hazards; in exposure to asbestos and organic solvents, for example, there are both short-term and long-term effects.

It can be difficult for researchers to accept that their research is not conclusive. Perhaps at best, TA can accurately analyze historical and current situations but is less reliable in predicting future trends.

Discussion

Although there is almost unanimous agreement on the need for TA, the reasons for this agreement vary. Noncritical approaches look to TA as a means of identifying potential resistance and assisting in a better social adjustment to technology. A critical feminist approach calls for an analysis of domination as a means of preventing exploitation of one group by another. Neither viewpoint regards the present situation as satisfactory. The one approach believes that social adaptation is too slow; the other, that the dissemination of technology is too fast and headed in the wrong direction.

I have drawn a major distinction between an approach to TA that is technology-oriented and one that is context-oriented: that is, it takes knowledge interests and the ensuing organization of use, treatment, and services into consideration. I have emphasized the need for methods that allow technology to be totally disregarded and a search for alternatives undertaken. This option further develops TA as an expression of a democratic learning process, with reference to decisions about what kind of technology and what sort of society are wanted. I advocate an ethical debate as a necessary supplement to TA. This is particularly crucial for those technologies that seriously challenge established social and cultural norms and values, such as new reproductive technology.

TA should be critical of the human needs that technology claims to meet. It should consider which social problems are the most pressing. The social context of technology could be defined from an alternative visionary presentation of technological and societal development. This opens the possibility for a political choice about what kind of goal is relevant for the technological development. In this way, a choice can be made with regard to development. In the meantime, the question becomes, what and which needs should be the basis for direction of development?

This criterion for a broad TA (at least in theory) opens the door for the integration of a woman's perspective. In practice, mainstream TA has made no attempt to include the study of the gender-specific impact of technology on women. Individual women and women representing a woman's perspective must be included in TA activities.

Much needs to be done. The list of criteria I have drawn up in Table 4 can be regarded as a blueprint for an ideal TA. It can also be seen as a checklist for areas that need to be developed further. I see an enormous task ahead in developing a more solid theoretical base for a critical feminist approach to TA, one that builds on theories of technology and society. I am one of those who believe that technological development—that is, the social context in which the innovations are developing—should be the starting point, but this approach needs to be strengthened both theoretically and methodologically. There is an urgent need for more empirical studies that can give accurate pictures of the situation today with regard to trends in technological development.

I perceive TA as a politically oriented tool, providing information about possible social consequences of technological development on several levels. It is important that the focus be on consequences based on needs. There is a very urgent need for empirical studies to identify the wants, needs, and desires of women with regard to the future of technological development.

I see a feminist approach to TA as having the potential to direct technology in such a way that it contributes to the autonomy of women in society. This approach calls for a systematic, continuous assessment of existing as well as emerging technology, done in the interests of and with the participation of women.

Technology is more than technique, so TA must do more than assess technique.

Notes
Bibliography
Index

Notes

Introduction

1. The environmental movement is one example.

2. In this study I use the concept "values" to represent ideas about what is desirable, proper, good, or bad; different or conflicting values represent aspects of variations between human groups.

3. I use the term "knowledge interests" to denote what Habermas (1972) calls "knowledge-constitutive interests." Put simply, this is the idea that knowledge is grounded in interest.

4. My criticism is aimed at institutionalized assessment, which I consider noncritical; however, non-institutionalized assessment, although most often critical in character, is also subject to criticism, especially when gender is ignored.

5. By "subordinate people," I mean those who lack autonomy and control over technological development and the use of technology that affects their lives at work, at home, or within society. Although I emphasize women's situation, using medical technology as an example, I see widespread general relevance for this analysis. After all, every human being—regardless of age, sex, race, or socioeconomic status—can instantaneously be put in the subordinate role of "patient."

6. It should be noted that a feminist perspective as such is not a set of prescriptive values. My definition of a feminist is a person who believes that women as a group are oppressed. Theoretically, there are several "feminist" interpretations and explanations for this oppression.

Chapter 1

1. The relationship between science and military power has its origins in ancient Greece and is a characteristic of Western science. This relationship intensified following World War II. According to Dickson (1984), the experiences of that war resulted in a rapid escalation of military force in both East and West, in which the application of

advanced scientific knowledge was used to produce weapons of mass destruction.

2. The mechanistic (also known as the Cartesian) paradigm is a way of seeing the world which maintains that all events or phenomena, no matter how complex, can ultimately be understood in a mechanical framework. This position is strongly deterministic and implicitly assumes the possibility of reductionism.

3. As pointed out by Jamison and Baark (1990, 124): "The original development of technology assessment as a concept was, to a large extent, a reaction to the critical social movements that developed in the 1960's and early 1970's. The pattern of using technology assessment to attempt to 'neutralize' or tame debate seems to be a recurring tendency."

4. This distinction is similar to that made by Jamison and Baark (1990) between two technology assessment trajectories: the practical and the theoretical.

5. "Luddism" is also used generically to describe the various kinds of machine-breaking by workers that have occurred since the disciples of King Ludd cracked looms and heads in the English Midlands.

6. In his book *Taming the Tiger*, Rybczynski (1983) offers recent examples, which include protesters holding a computer "hostage." Individual protest, more difficult to document, is exemplified by women who, in protest at having to work on word-processing machines all day, have been known to spill hot coffee or tiny sugar tablets into the keyboards (Morgall 1982c). Examples from the field of medicine are civil suits brought by individual women against major drug companies, claiming damage as a result of taking birth control pills.

7. Examples are the nuclear accident at Three Mile Island in 1979 in the United States and the Chernobyl accident in the Soviet Union in April 1986.

8. Asbestos is a very dangerous material used in industry since the turn of the century in thermal and acoustic insulation, fireproofing, fiber-reinforcing construction, shipbuilding, demolition, and the auto industry. Even limited exposures have been shown to cause, in the long term, fibrosis of the lungs (asbestosis) and various cancers. As early as 1930 asbestos use was made illegal in some parts of the world; however, the call for a total ban as well as the exposure of new cases received the greatest publicity throughout the 1960s and 1970s (Kinnersly 1974).

9. In 1978 a Danish report claimed that aromatic epoxy resins, used extensively in the shipbuilding industry, correlated highly with carcinomas. Workplace exposure also identified epoxy as the cause of eczema and allergies. Following the release of this report, workers in the shipbuilding industry went on strike for several months (Morgall 1980).

10. The most damaging side effect is the increased risk of blood clots, though little research has actually been done into the detrimental effects of birth control pills over time.

11. Thalidomide, a drug frequently used during the 1950s as a treatment for nausea in pregnancy, was later associated with congenital malformation of the fetus.

12. Approximately 85 percent of the British and American resources devoted to R&D is spent on work done in industry or govern-

ment establishments. Since over 90 percent of these funds come from industry or government, clearly these institutions play the dominant role in determining the rate and direction of technical change (Coombs, Saviotti, and Walsh 1987).

13. For a detailed analysis of the political forces working for and against institutionalizing assessment of the social impacts of science and technology, see Dickson (1984).

14. OTA still keeps a peace political line with information, for example, about the possible consequences of atomic war.

15. An example of a public health issue was an investigation into the effects of lead poisoning, which revealed that about 400,000 children were affected annually, with 200 deaths each year as a result, by ingesting thirty-year-old lead-based paint. The question was raised whether Congress could have anticipated this problem and enacted legislation to prevent it (Gibbons and Gwin 1988).

16. The top five priorities of OTA in 1979 were the impact of technology on national water supply and demand, alternative global food futures, health promotion and disease prevention, technology and world population, and the impact of technology on land productivity.

17. The original members were Austria, Belgium, Canada, Denmark, France, the Federal Republic of Germany, Greece, Iceland, Ireland, Italy, Luxembourg, the Netherlands, Norway, Portugal, Spain, Sweden, Switzerland, Turkey, the United Kingdom and the United States; they were later joined by Japan, Finland, Australia, and New Zealand.

18. For example, the Delphi Technique, originated by the U.S. military to collect and synthesize expert opinions concerning defense issues, is still basic to the military decision-making process (see Chapter 3).

19. The idea that social movements and pressure groups play a significant part in society is related to the concept of pluralism, since the political process is seen to result from a large number of often competing pressures.

20. Kuhn's *Structure of Scientific Revolution* (1970) renewed interest in the debate about the origin and growth of modern science.

21. The early 1960s have been referred to as the period of rediscovering the sociological conceptions of knowledge (Eyerman and Jamison 1991). This rediscovery challenged the limited and highly fragmented views of knowledge that had dominated the postwar era.

22. This was true of Sally Hacker (1989), a sociologist and organizer who studied the effects of technology on women in various fields: telecommunications, agribusiness, printing and publishing, and insurance.

23. Gartner (1982) sees this power as being expressed in many ways: the consumer protection movement; the environmentalists; demands for community control and the involvement of consumers on community boards; the expansion of the rights of all groups, including minorities, welfare recipients, the aged, people with disabilities, tenants, prisoners, women, homosexuals.

24. The Public Interest Research Group run by Ralph Nader has successfully challenged the U.S. government and large corporations over such issues as car safety, food additives, and the withholding of information (in the 1960s and 1970s, newspapers and scandal sheets

often reported stories of threats to Nader's life from large corporations). One successful campaign launched in the United States was to remove lead from gasoline (Coombs, Saviotti, and Walsh 1987).

25. One example in the United Kingdom is the Lucas Aero Space Joint Shop Stewards' Alternative Corporate plan. When Lucas was faced with the necessity of rationalization and cutbacks, the workforce opposed redundancy and proposed diversification instead, presenting detailed designs and specifications for products suited to the firm's facilities and equipment. This effort, however, met resistance from the company, which saw it as a threat to management's prerogative to direct operations and make decisions (Cooley 1980).

26. Examples can be found in OECD's activities and publications on public participation in decisions related to science and technology (OECD 1979), and OTA's numerous attempts to include the public in consensus conferences.

Chapter 2

1. Asbestos was first mined before 1900, but not until 1930 was exposure to the material recognized as hazardous. In 1931 regulations were introduced in Britain. In 1955 exposure to asbestos particles was recognized as a cause of lung cancer and in the mid-1960s as the cause of a rare pleural cancer. In 1969 amendments were made to the 1931 regulations and further amendments in 1984 (Coombs, Saviotti, and Walsh 1987).

2. Epidemiology is the study of the incidence and distribution of diseases and illness in the human population. In medical sociology it involves the study of how factors such as social class, age, sex, and culture influence the presence of illness (Abercrombie 1988).

3. Exceptions were those whose main objective was to examine the EC's potential for action.

4. This can be explained by the special relationship between the Congress and the office of the American president. In most European countries, the central administration plays a different role in legislative work than it does in the United States. The tendency in these countries has been to attach technology assessment work to the administration, as was done in Sweden.

5. The OTA is run by the Technology Assessment Board (TAB), which consists of six members of the two houses of Congress (elected officials), and a director (who has no vote). TAB is supplemented by the Technology Advisory Council, which consists of experts in various fields. The procedure allows any member of Congress to approach TAB and request that a particular problem be examined.

6. Sweden, the Netherlands, France, and West Germany requested their parliaments to establish a technology assessment institute similar to the OTA, but none of the four did so.

7. I define implicit TA as an attempt to integrate assessment into larger programs of science and technology or industrial policy; most often, there is no specific or separate budget for TA activities.

8. The Commission Nationale d'Homologation approves recently developed technologies, reviewing the results of tests before the technology is made available to the public. The Comité d'Evaluation et de Diffusion de l'Innovation Technologique has produced assessment reports. The Transferance et Evaluation Prototypes is a procedure cre-

ated under the Ministry of Industry to assist industry even before the development phase by helping to produce prototypes, find experimentation sites, and write and disseminate assessment reports on potential innovations.

9. This independent body is the Nederlandse Organisatie voor Technologisch Aspekten Onderzoek.

10. See, e.g., the extensive review of technology assessment as practiced in Europe prepared by the Dutch Ministry of Education and Science (Dutch Ministry 1987), as well as the report on anticipating and assessing health care technology prepared for the Dutch Ministry of Health (STG 1987).

11. The concept of "partisan research" is discussed in more detail in Chapter 4.

12. It should be noted that this influence can be attributed to the social and professional status physicians enjoy in most countries. As professionals who specialize in the development of technical knowledge, and come in daily contact with issues of life and death which affect everyone, they acquire the power of definition and the authority to determine what constitutes "normal" physical and mental states. Eliot Freidson (1980) analyzed this power and the subsequent control using theories of professionalism. Of particular interest to feminists is medical knowledge used as a means to control the human body (as in cases of reproductive technology) and to medicalize normal life events such as menstruation, childbearing, and menopause.

13. Third-party payers are usually state or private insurance programs.

14. In 1984 the European member states of WHO signed a commitment to the thirty-eight targets that were agreed upon as part of the global program "Health for All by the Year 2000." Target 38 deals with health technology and its effectiveness, efficiency, safety, and acceptability.

15. STG stands for Stuurgroep Toekomstscenario's Gezondheidzorg, established as an independent advisory group to the State Secretary for Welfare, Public Health, and Cultural Affairs.

16. Previously, the assessment of medical devices, equipment, and procedures had been conducted through the Swedish Planning and Rationalization Institute of Health Studies (SPRI).

17. The Australian National Health Technology Advisory Panel was established in 1982 (IJTAHC 1989).

18. One could argue that wide-scale problems related to technology, such as pollution, have also been a problem in Eastern Europe, where until recently there was no way to monitor public protest.

19. This is an observation I have made repeatedly in my research in the health care sector, most recently in the project "Samarbejde mellem Brugerorganisationer & Apoteksfarmaceuter om Lægemiddelanvendelse" (Cooperation between patient associations and pharmacists with regard to drug use) (Hansen, Launsoe, and Morgall 1989). There are many patients' associations in Denmark, and only a few are "pure": i.e., not run by health care professionals.

20. Because their primary goal is to make (save) money, private insurers and government programs that pay a provider for care given to a patient have been responsible for cutting of hospital stays and establishing payment ceilings for various medical treatments and pro-

cedures—particularly in the United States, where there is no national health care insurance.

21. It should be noted that the women's health movement has been most visible in its activist form in the United States, the United Kingdom, and Italy, though as a subject of research and educational interest it has been wide-spread throughout the Western world. Curiously, it never took root in Scandinavia as a critical grassroots movement. I attribute this to the "sacred cow" status the health care system has (until recently) enjoyed there. In the 1970s and 1980s Scandinavian health care was a "model" for Western, non-Communist countries, and proud Scandinavians—believing they had the best health care system in the world—were reluctant to criticize it.

22. Another relevant issue in the discussion of medicalization is the establishment as routine of such procedures as ultrasound scanning of all pregnant women (Koch and Morgall 1987).

23. DES is a synthetic estrogen that was frequently given to pregnant women from the 1940s to 1950s in the belief that it prevented miscarriage. Although it was tested in controlled clinical trials, it was never proved effective in preventing miscarriage but has been found to cause cancer and other severe problems, both in the women who were given the drug and in their offspring, particularly daughters. It is still in use as a "morning after" contraceptive (Klein 1989).

24. The medical industry produces an overwhelming amount of literature, not just for the purpose of advertising but also in the "guise" of scientific research: that is, manufacturers fund medical research that specifically uses their products. It is not unusual that this literature is not critical. The critique of medical research by Ratcliff (1989) in the discussion of a feminist perspective takes up this point.

25. See, e.g., Stanworth (1987) and Seal (1990). For an analysis of the feminist debate on new reproductive technology, see Wajcman (1991) and Vanderwater (1992).

Chapter 3

1. The Dutch study on future health scenarios, conducted in the 1980s (STG 1987), is an exception.

2. In Japan an entire industry tries to plan its future development with the use of new technology (Meyer 1991). In the United States, however, it is felt that this form of cooperation between companies does not follow the rules of competition. Moreover, constructive TA requires time, perhaps a five-year period, whereas U.S. stockholders are not usually willing to wait longer than three months to realize profits.

3. Starr's (1972) risk-benefit analysis for skiing bases the estimate for fatalities per exposure hour on information obtained from the National Ski Patrol for the 1967–68 southern California ski season: 1 fatality, 17 days of skiing, 16,500 skiers per day, and 5 hours of skiing per skier per day. The estimate of benefit is based on the average number of days of skiing per year per person and the average cost of a typical ski trip, plus an average expenditure per skier of $25 per year for equipment.

Chapter 4

1. One exception is France. In the early 1980s the Socialist government (headed by François Mitterand) gave priority to technological

development and attempted to formulate a technology policy to strengthen the French computer industry in its struggle against U.S. and Japanese competition. The plan included state-supported social experiments (carried out on regional labor markets), emphasis on education in the computer sciences, and huge telecommunication projects (Vedel 1986).

2. An exception is the project carried out by the Commission on Future Health Technology in the Netherlands, which has produced several reports for the Ministry of Health, among them one on anticipating and assessing health care technology (STG 1987). These cannot be considered long-term societal goals, however, but must be more narrowly defined as long-term health goals.

3. The situation was provoked by the Danish environmental movement's militant rejection of a nuclear energy plant, one of the most effective campaigns in the world: there are still no nuclear energy plants in Denmark, and the movement's trademark, a sticker with a brightly colored sun and the words *Atomkraft . . . Nej tak!* (Nuclear energy . . . No thanks), became the symbol of the anti-nuclear movement in the West.

4. In the end, however, the council was persuaded to make an economic assessment.

5. In an example from Denmark, a new drug reimbursement policy was initiated, the so-called 800 DKK rule, in the state's attempt to save on the health care budget. The Ministry of Health authorized several assessment projects to evaluate the effect of this rule. Suddenly, after a few months and as a result of public pressure, the rule was discontinued and the assessment projects informed that their funding had been stopped and they therefore should discontinue the assessment. This upset the short-term plans of research institutes that had committed time and personnel to this endeavor.

6. This was the case in Denmark from 1982 to 1993. The Social Democrats are the largest single party in Parliament, but were unable to form a coalition until 1993. The coalition formed by the right never had a stable majority, and the threat of a new election was always looming, prior to every important political decision that came up for a vote in Parliament.

7. Translation by the author; emphasis added.

8. As noted in Chapter 1, a contributing factor to the establishment of the OTA was that legislators felt they could not rely on "expert" testimony, which they found to be contradictory and biased.

9. Except for research done within industry, TA research is often dependent on outside funding. Private industry and public agencies are the main sources. It is difficult to imagine purely altruistic and non-political motives on the part of either these funding agencies *or* the recipients of the funds.

10. Professionals (i.e., experts), physicians as well as scientists, often join special interest groups as private persons. Whether forming their own special professional interest group or becoming part of an already established group (such as a patient association or environmental group), their specialized knowledge often gives them status and, thereby, power both within the group and as outside spokespersons for it.

11. Doing so is linked to the problems associated with access to information and the hiring of experts discussed in Chapter 2.

12. I know of one woman who, in the 1980s, acted for years as the "consumer representative" at World Health Organization meetings on a variety of medical issues. Her original expertise was as a member of a consumer group involved in childbirth concerns. After gaining experience as an outspoken consumer at a meeting on that topic, she went on to represent the unsuspecting public at meetings about everything from drug consumption to psychiatric problems.

13. "Partisan research" and "partisan TA" are terms used to refer to the two parties (partners) of the labor market: employers and employees. I apply the concept to all parties (or partners) in technological development, acknowledging the existence of different and often conflicting interests between the various parties.

14. For example, a group of citizens in a housing project can have an opinion on building technology which is not necessarily in the interest of either the employer or employees. Similarly, citizens in a consumer group can have an opinion on additives in food that is not necessarily compatible with the interest of either partner in the labor market (Moeller 1986).

15. This was characteristic of phase two TA, discussed in Chapter 2. Although there was a will to do multidisciplinary assessment, taking social and human consequences into consideration, the only people with experience in TA were technicians, engineers, and economists. Their approach and methods were technical, rational, and economic, focusing on the technology itself with no consideration for alternative solutions. It took years to get the views of social scientists introduced, and it is questionable whether they have ever been widely accepted.

16. The three subcommittees were each to consist of a representative from the labor unions, a representative from management (the employers' association), and one from the so-called "professional organizations and grassroots groups" (social movements).

17. This argument is characteristic of an approach that ignores conflict and contradiction and believes in neutral TA.

18. For example, how can a noise level of 90 decibels be measured against an investment savings of one million dollars?

19. In the second report of the Technology Council was a progress report on the organization of TA in Denmark which included experiences and perspectives (Teknologistyrelsen 1984). It was strongly criticized within the research community because the board did not define what it meant by technology.

20. Theory-based TA has been particularly prevalent in Denmark as a result of the Teknik-Samfund Initiativet, funded by the Social Sciences Research Council. Even in Denmark, however, MTA is predominantly void of explicit theoretical underpinnings.

Chapter 5

1. Carried to the limits, the social constructionist analysis of science is extreme sociological reductionism: all knowledge becomes reducible to the interests of the group that produces it (Rose 1987).

2. In this context, "labor process" is defined as the means by which raw materials are transformed by human labor (acting on the objects with tools and machinery) first into products for use and, under capitalism, into commodities to be exchanged on the market (Thompson 1983).

3. See, e.g., the work of Barker and Downing (1980), Cockburn (1986, 1987), Cowan (1985), Wajcman (1991).

4. See esp. the work of Harry Braverman (1974), which was at the center of the labor process debate.

5. It should also be mentioned that women were not the only ones excluded during the formative days of science and later on. Money, class, race, social status, and geographic divisions within society and between various countries have always limited access to the study and practice of science.

6. There is a wealth of literature on this topic, including feminist critiques of the state under various systems: capitalism, welfare states, socialism, communism. I restrict myself to discussions of the state's role in technology assessment (see Part I), specifically in the United States and Western Europe.

7. The regulating role of the state is of special importance in labor negotiations and in health services financed by public funds, two sectors where technology has had a tremendous impact.

8. In the social sciences, feminist analysis developed as an extension of the critique launched by the radical science movement of the 1960s, which viewed science as an instrument of war and class oppression (Rose 1982) but, like the labor process debates, ignored gender.

9. See Acker (1989) for a detailed account of the problem with the concept of patriarchy in the development of feminist thought.

10. For example, contemporary theories of patriarchy developed by psychoanalytical feminists attempted to explain patriarchy by using the theories of Freud and his followers (Chodorow 1978; Dinnerstein 1976; Kittay 1984). They emphasize the emotional dynamics of personality and emotions that are often deeply buried in the subconscious or unconscious of the psyche.

11. I refer the reader to Young (1981) and Vedel (1986) for a discussion of the debate on single versus dual systems theory.

12. The differences lie in their interpretation of which elements patriarchy encompasses. For example, one defines patriarchy as itself a mode of production that interacts with the capitalist mode of production. Another defines patriarchy as an ideological psychological system that interacts with material relations in society.

13. In sociology the concept of the division of labor is analyzed in three ways: the technical division of labor, which describes the production process; the social division of labor, which refers to the differentiation in society as a whole; and the sexual division of labor, which describes the social division between men and women (Abercrombie, Hill, and Turner 1988).

14. In Denmark in the 1980s, unskilled workers and subordinate functionaries constituted 67 percent of all working women but only 39 percent of men (Ligestillingsraadet 1987).

15. In the United States in 1985, only 15 percent of middle management positions were filled by women. The figure for Scandinavia (Denmark, Norway, and Sweden) was approximately 5 percent (Morgall and Vedel 1985).

16. Mumford's language should be seen within the context of the technology literature available at that time, which was totally male dominated.

17. E.g., Mike Cooley (1980) not only argues for human-centered

technologies but advocates developing technology based on women's values. Arnold Pacey (1983) also deals with women's values in discussing the culture of technology.

18. This theme corresponds to (and at times can be seen as an extension of) the critiques done in the 1960s and 1970s on the limitations of science and technology.

19. In this literature, we find the explanation that the origin of gender roles is the hierarchic split between men, women, and nature. According to Gray (1979), the Genesis creation story is male myth establishing a hierarchic dualism that places God and men above, women and nature below.

20. Merchant perceives the domination of nature (and of women) as license for an aggressive and exploitive market economy.

21. The concept of masculinity as a value was examined by Paul Willis (1979) in a study of young men in the United Kingdom. He found masculinity an important factor in understanding working-class culture. Investigating why young men voluntarily accept manual labor, Willis found that they reinterpret the brutality of the work situation as a heroic exercise of manly confrontation with the task. In fact, throughout his study, Willis shows patriarchy to be the pivot around which capitalism turns.

22. See also Braverman's (1974) analysis of scientific management and the introduction of the factory system.

23. The humanities define culture as the common world of experience shared by a group of people, which in turn forms their ethics, values, and ways of relating to the world they live in.

24. This has been called the "add women and stir" recipe for improvement.

25. In the same study, girls who had chosen natural science and technology had, to a very high degree, an especially strong relationship with their fathers. They had often had a "boy upbringing" more than a "girl upbringing" (sometimes because there were no boys in the family) and a lot of help and support from their fathers with regard to education.

26. This finding is similar to that of Kvande (1982).

27. This is also the trend in engineering education. In 1991 the number of females entering the Technical University of Denmark was 20.5 percent of total admissions, as compared to 22.5 percent the year before.

28. This sentiment is often found in the social constructionist literature: see, e.g., the collection of works by MacKenzie and Wajcman (1987).

29. The point is documented in Noble's recent work (1992b), which traces the masculine field of science back to the celibate Christian clerical tradition of the Middle Ages.

Chapter 6

1. I have encountered the same problems when teaching a course in medical sociology to pharmacy students. They have a difficult time understanding that there is no single accepted and correct theory of the role of medicine in society but, in fact, several theories (and various approaches), which interpret the phenomenon in different ways.

2. Bush's model consists of a two-dimensional diagram of a wheel with four concentric circles. The technology to be assessed is placed at the hub of the wheel. Spokes radiate outward to carry the four primary effects (in the second circle) to the third and outermost levels. Multiple effects can be incorporated: the number of segments within each circle can be increased to include additional effects at each level. The completed diagram is a visual representation that allows one to "contemplate several different variables or relationships at the same time" (Bush 1981), in contrast to a linear progression model, which can move only from one order of effects to another, without being able to show interaction.

3. In nonfeminist literature, this "myth" is called technological determinism, which among other beliefs supports the view of technology as a positive sign of human progress.

4. *Silent Spring* was a book written in nontechnical language (it appeared in installments in the *New Yorker* magazine prior to publication), which criticized the pesticide industry. Carson argued that synthetic poisons (1) ignore realities of biology and create worse insect problems than the original problem, and (2) cause drift (see note 5). The book had a tremendous impact on public opinion; thirty years later, it still serves as an inspiration for major environmental programs, which base their spending decisions on evaluation of the phenomena Carson depicted.

5. "Drift" is a term adapted by Hynes from the tendency of chemical pesticides, when sprayed, to drift beyond the areas at which they were directed, thereby causing unintended damage to neighboring life, both plant and animal.

6. I find this to be a general characteristic of medical research based on the "medical model" and therefore applicable to both men and women.

7. This can be seen as a consequence of the mechanistic paradigm (Merchant 1980) discussed in Chapter 5, which was encouraged through the growth and spread of medical specialties. Specialization today has gone so far that hospital departments are divided according to parts of the body.

8. I am aware that considerable research has been done on technological development using critical theory (in Denmark especially), but this is the exception and not the rule. All in all, an overwhelming body of TA (and especially MTA) research is characterized by a technological deterministic approach.

9. For a collection of old and new articles gathered under the heading of social constructionist theories, see *The Social Shaping of Technology* (MacKenzie and Wajcman 1987).

10. "Culture lag" is the perceived inability of society to keep up with technological change.

11. In tropical medicine, for example, solutions are desperately needed to control and cure various diseases. The "problem" is defined, the "need" is there, but no one has yet found the appropriate solution (Herborg 1989).

12. "The introduction of a discipline's paradigm or a 'school's' paradigm occurs over a period of many years of the education or socialization process in which a personality is formed and the intellectual skills are linked to relationships that are emotional and value-laden. In

an interdisciplinary research team, when a person is face to face with
another researcher who has a paradigm that is different from his or her
own, the foreign paradigm intrudes and can challenge a person's own
foundations and self-image" (Launsoe and Rieper 1987, 120; my translation).

13. This has been a problem in my own research, where I often
work with health care professionals whose training is in natural science. For explanations, see Ratcliff's (1989) example of medical doctors
as assessors, Freidson's (1970, 1980) theory of professions, and by Launsoe and Rieper's (1987) example of interdisciplinary cooperation. Medical professionals can become defensive when participating in multidisciplinary research projects that analyze *their* place or mode of work,
and that involve professionals in other fields who use research theory
and methods unknown to them.

Chapter 7

1. Bevan's analysis divides the literature on secretaries and office
technology into what he calls three research "schools": managerialist,
sociotechnical, and humanistic. I prefer the term "approach" to define
the entry point—including the assumptions from which these studies
are conducted—because many of these authors are only implicitly doing what I would term research; they are not consciously aware of following any research theory or tradition. Another reason is that Bevan,
not the authors themselves, has chosen to put them into these categories

2. Jobs that disappear by natural attrition are jobs that people
have left (that is, they were not fired or made redundant) because of
retirement, a new job, long-term illness, or death.

3. In a study of women in organizations, Kanter (1977) compiled
a list of criteria that she found equally relevant to the relationship between men and their wives and that between men and their secretaries.

4. Their study looks at the evolution of the subservient role of the
secretary and its perpetuation by sexual stereotyping.

5. Launsoe's criteria for a "subject perspective" require that researchers listen to participants; establish a dialogue with participants;
and, when possible, empower participants.

6. These issues were being openly debated in the United Kingdom and the United States, where this technology was already spread-
ing rapidly (e.g., Harman 1974; APEX 1979).

7. "Simple control" is a term adopted by Edwards (1979) in his
historical analysis of control systems in the workplace. As opposed to
technical and bureaucratic control, it is based on the direct personal
authority of managers or employers.

8. This study was done in West Yorkshire, U.K., between 1980
and 1985.

9. The best-paid respondents were those involved in purchasing
and other traditionally managerial roles. At senior management level,
average earnings were over 80 percent higher than those of middle
managers, but the few women at senior management levels were, on
the average, paid less than male middle managers: "It is a $5,000 a year
liability to be a woman in software . . . the field is not characterized by
just random pay discrepancies but by systematic pay discrimination
against women" (Kraft and Dubnoff 1984).

10. Burris builds on the work of organizational control done by Edwards (1979). The significance of her study is twofold: (1) she updates what she sees as a series of different types of workplace control—precapitalist craft/guild control, simple control, technical control, bureaucratic control, and professionalism—and introduces the concept of "technocratic control"; (2) she adds a gender analysis to the discussion of organizational control.

11. Other characteristics defined by Burris include the declining importance of internal job ladders in favor of external credentialization and credential barriers; the increased importance of technical expertise as a central basis of organizational authority; the transformation of professionals and managers into specialized experts concerned with administration and efficiency; and the emergence of a worldwide technocratic system.

12. Kraft and Dubnoff (1984) reported similar results in an earlier survey.

13. Remote-based work for women is not new; for example, home sewing has been a common job for women since the early 1900s.

14. The examples of remote-based work that already exist in the United States, United Kingdom, Germany, Sweden, and France clearly show that this method of organizing work affects, first and foremost, women who do routine office tasks. To date, it has been the rule rather than the exception that ancillary tasks are carried out in the home or in neighborhood work centers, while decision-making and planning continue to take place centrally (Elling 1984; Vedel 1986; Vedel and Morgall 1982).

15. Bevan (1985) came closest, but his study was not designed to examine the issues from the users' perspective.

16. Even a high level of unionization (as in Scandinavia) does not mean that union members are active. The very nature of clerical work—low-level, part-time, etc.—can be seen as a factor contributing to the nonmilitancy of this group of workers.

17. This point was made earlier in this chapter in the discussion of the history of clerical work and the recruitment of women from the middle classes to fill clerical jobs.

Chapter 8

1. Exceptions are vasectomies and condoms, which have in no way been issues as controversial as abortion, birth control pills, IVF, etc.

2. I have written about this topic in Denmark from a historical perspective (Morgall and Rasmussen 1987).

3. Hormonal contraceptives are artificially synthesized derivatives of the natural steroid hormones estrogen and progesterone.

4. This paradigm views disease as caused by a specific etiological agent known as the "disease entity."

5. Restoring health in a body conceptualized as a machine with functional parts requires the use of tools in the form of medical technology and advanced scientific procedures.

6. See, e.g., methodological critiques by a medical sociologist (Oakley 1990); and by a pharmacist and a sociologist (Hansen and Launsoe 1989).

7. The "medical profession" is the term used to describe the persons performing the role of doctor or physician in modern society. In

most countries, they enjoy a high social standing as well as relatively higher incomes than persons in many other professions. The exclusive possession of knowledge is a powerful weapon, and the medical profession practices what Friedson (1970) calls "boundary maintenance": it seeks to maintain a monopoly on the knowledge skills its members acquire during their training, while trying to prevent other groups from exploiting to the full the value of the knowledge they possess.

8. This is the case of IVF treatment; it use is not based totally on medical criteria but includes other exclusion criteria (see the following section).

9. At the time, Lene Koch was a research fellow at the Institute of General Practice, University of Copenhagen, and was writing a dissertation on women's experiences with IVF.

10. IVF is still considered experimental by the World Health Organization (Wagner 1986), as well as in many countries in the world.

11. I was told by a physician at a recent meeting in Copenhagen that the "real reason" IVF so quickly became "standard treatment" in Denmark was an administrative decision: had the IVF program remained "experimental," it would have been dependent on outside funding, which would have placed the continuity of the program in jeopardy. Defining it as standard treatment placed it within the hospital's normal budget.

12. The implications include artificial wombs, cloning, aspirating and freezing eggs to be used at a later time (among other reasons, to avoid pollution or radiation damage to genetic quality), and even the extreme possibility of allowing a man to carry a child to term after IVF and implantation in the abdominal cavity (Corea 1985).

13. Cf. the previous mention of the use of fetal tissue in the treatment of Parkinson's disease.

14. We lack scientific knowledge on the effects of ultrasound on oocytes, the psychological and physiological effects of the hormones used to superovulate, and the effects of the anesthesia necessary.

15. This figure was reported by CNN on October 23, 1991.

16. At a meeting of feminist academics on reproductive technology, a colleague who presented a paper on the oppressive aspects of IVF treatment for women reported that she was accused of not showing solidarity with infertile women.

17. The results of a recent interview study I conducted on repeat abortions (Osler, Morgall, and Jensen 1990) showed that the most frequent reasons women give for choosing an abortion are based on material considerations. Often they give a combination of reasons that appear to be concrete, not emotional or based on feelings.

18. One publicized case was that of a brain-dead mother who was kept alive in an effort to save the life of a four-month old fetus (*Washington Post*, December 2, 1977).

19. "Technological imperative" is a term coined by Fuchs (1968) to suggest that the addition of any new technology generates further use by its very existence and, in turn, generates still more technology.

20. These two procedures are good examples of how technology "creeps" into standard care. Both were originally developed as diagnostic tools to be used when there was a definite risk to the woman and/or the fetus. Yet ultrasound scanning is now standard procedure, and amniocentesis is standard for a particular age group (usually over thirty-

five, but the age is being lowered to include more and more women). These procedures cannot be considered risk-free (Koch and Morgall 1987).

21. This theory is supported by the recent work of David Noble (1992b), who writes of village women orally passing on knowledge of magic and herbal law from generation to generation.

22. These are equivalent to what Boman (1981) calls "solidarity and caring."

Bibliography

Aas, Berit. 1975. On female culture: An attempt to formulate a theory of women's solidarity and action. *Acta Sociologica* 18.2–3:142–61.

Abercrombie, Nicholas, Stephen Hill, and Bryan S. Turner. 1988. *The Penguin dictionary of sociology*. Penguin, London.

Acker, Joan. 1989. The problem with patriarchy. *Sociology* 23.2:235–40.

Alic, Margaret. 1981. Women and technology in ancient Alexandria. *Women's Studies International Quarterly* 4.3:305–12.

APEX (Association of Professional Executive, Clerical, and Computer Staff). 1979. *Office technology: The trade union response*. APEX, London.

———. 1982. *Office automation and the office worker*. Office Technology Working Party, London.

Arbejdsmarkedsnaevnet. 1990. *Fremtidens krav til kontoransatte i den offentlige sektor*. Arbejdsmarkedsnaevnet, Copenhagen.

Arditti, Rita. 1979. Feminism and science. In *Science and liberation*, ed. Rita Arditti, P. Brennan, and S. Cavrak. South End Press, Boston.

Arnold, Erik, and Wendy Faulkner. 1985. Smothered by invention: The masculinity of technology. In *Smothered by invention: Technology in women's lives*, ed. Wendy Faulkner and Erik Arnold. Pluto, London.

Bahrdt, Hans-Paul. 1958. *Industriebürokratie, versuch einer soziologie des industrialisierten bürobetriebes und seiner angestellten*. Enke, Stuttgart.

Banta, David H., Clyde J. Behney, and Jane Sisk Willems. 1981. *Toward rational technology in medicine*. Springer, New York.

Baram, Michael S. 1973. Technology assessment and social control. *Science* 180 (May 4): 465–73.

Barker, J., and H. Downing. 1980. Word processing and the transformation of patriarchal relations of control in the office. *Capital and Class* 10 (Spring): 64–99.

Baxandall, Rosalyn, Elizabeth Ewen, and Linda Gordon. 1976. The working class has two sexes. In *Technology: The labor process and the working class*. Monthly Review Press, New York.

Ben-David, J., and A. Zloczower. 1972. The growth of industrialized science in Germany. In *Sociology of science*, ed. B. Barnes. Penguin, Harmondsworth.

Benet, Mary Kathleen. 1973. *The secretarial ghetto*. McGraw-Hill, New York.

Berg, M., and D. Michael. 1978. *Factors affecting utilization of technology assessment studies in policy making*. Institute for Social Research, University of Michigan, Ann Arbor.

Bergom-Larsson, Maria. 1982. Women and technology in the industrialized countries. In *Scientific-technological changes and the role of women in development*, ed. Pamela M. D'Onofrio-Flores and Sheila M. Pfafflin. Westview Press, Boulder, Colo.

Bermann, Tamar. 1988. Feministisk Teknologidebatt paa amerikansk. *Nyt om Kvinneforskning*, May, pp. 14–21.

Berner, Boel. 1975. *Kvinnor innen teknik och naturvetenskap*. University of Lund, Lund.

——. 1982. Kvinnor: Kunskap och makt i teknikens värld. *Kvinnovetenskaplig Tidskrift*, no. 3:25–39.

——. 1984. New technology and women's education in Sweden. In *World yearbook of education 1984: Women and education*, ed. Sandra Acker, Jacquetta Megarry, Stanley Nisbet, and Eric Hoyle. Kogan Page, London.

——. 1985. Women, power, and ideology in technical education and work. Paper presented to the International Conference on the Role of Women in the History of Science, Technology, and Medicine in the Nineteenth and Twentieth Centuries. VESzprém, Hungary.

Bevan, Stephen M. 1985. *Secretaries and typists: The impact of office automation*. Report 93. Institute of Manpower Studies, Brighton.

——. 1987. New office technology and the changing role of secretaries. In *Women and information technology*, ed. M. J. Davidson and C. L. Cooper. Wiley, New York.

Bird, E. 1980. *Information technology in the office: The impact on women's jobs*. Equal Opportunities Commission, Manchester, U.K.

Birke, Lynda, Wendy Faulkner, and Kathy Ovenfield. 1980. *Alice through the microscope: The power of science over women's lives*. Virago, London.

Bjoern-Andersen, N., M. Earl, O. Holst, and E. Mumford. eds. 1982. *Information society: For richer, for poorer*. Elsevier, Amsterdam.

Bliven, Bruce. 1954. *The wonderful writing machine*. Random House, New York.

Boman, Anne. 1981. Omsorg och solidaritet—ohaallbara argument. *Kvinnovetenskapligtidskrift* 1–2:51–54.

Borchorst, Anette. 1984. *Arbejdsmarkedets koensopdeling: Patriarkalsk dominans eller kvinders valg?* Aalborg University, Aalborg.

Bose, Christine, et al. 1988. Teaching women and technology. *Women's International Quarterly* 4.3:295–304.

Bowles, Samuel, and Richard Edwards. 1985. *Understanding capitalism, competition, command, and change in the U.S. economy*. Harper & Row, New York.

Braendgaard, Asger. 1983. Teknologivurdering. *Smaaskrift*, no. 50, side 12. Aalborg University Center, AUC, Aalborg.

Braverman, Harry. 1974. *Labor and monopoly capital: The degradation of work in the twentieth century.* Monthly Review Press, New York.

Breugel, I. 1979. Women as a reserve army of labor: A note on recent British experience. *Feminist Review* 3:12–23.

Brook, Robert. 1986. Technology assessment. Paper presented at the Workshop on Methods for Technology Assessment in Primary Health Care, Copenhagen.

Brooks, Harvey. 1973. Technology assessment as a process. *International Social Science Journal* 25.3:247.

———. 1976. Technology assessment in retrospect. *Newsletter on Science, Technology, and Human Values*, no. 17 (October): 17–29.

———. 1988. Controlling technology: Risks, costs, and benefits. In *Technology and politics*, ed. Michael E. Kraft and Norman J. Vig. Duke University Press, Durham, N.C.

Brorsson, Bengt, and Stig Wall. 1985. *Assessment of medical technology: Problems and methods.* Swedish Medical Research Council, Falun.

Bruce, Margaret, and Alison Adams. 1989. Expert systems and women's lives: A technology assessment. *Futures*, October, pp. 480–97.

Bruvik-Hansen, A., Y. Billing, and L. B. Rasmussen. 1983. *Kvinders Forhold til Ingenioeruddannelserne.* Institut for Samfundsfag, Danmarks Tekniske Højskole, Lygby.

Buchanan, D. A., and D. Boddy. 1982. Advanced technology and the quality of working life: The effects of word processing on the videotypists. *Journal of Occupational Psychology* 55:1–11.

Buch Andreasen, Per. 1988. *Ugeskrift* 150.13 (March 28): 823–25.

Burris, Beverly H. 1983. *No room at the top: Under-employment and alienation in the corporation.* Praeger, New York.

———. 1989. Technocratic organization and gender. *Women's Studies International Forum* 12.4:447–62.

Bush, Corlann Gee. 1981. *Taking hold of technology: Topic guide for 1981–83.* American Association of University Women, Washington, D.C.

———. 1983. Women and the assessment of technology: To think, to be, to unthink, to free. In *Machina ex dea: Feminist perspectives on technology*, ed. Joan Rothschild. Pergamon, Elmsford, N.Y.

———. 1987. Dethroning technology. *Women's Review of Books* 4.12 (September): 13.

Capra, Fritjof. 1986. Wholeness and health. *Holistic Medicine* 1:145–59.

Carson, Rachel. 1962. *The silent spring.* Houghton Mifflin, Boston.

Chodorow, Nancy. 1978. *The reproduction of mothering: Psychoanalysis and the sociology of gender.* University of California Press, Berkeley.

Christensen, Jytte Moeller, and Helga Sigmund. 1986. *Informationssystemer, teknologivurdering og sundhedstjeneste.* Roskilde University Center, Tek-Sam, Roskilde.

Christmas-Moeller, Ingeborg. 1984. Havsvampe, the, P-piller og vaccine. Om praevention gennem tiderne. *Forum for Kvindeforskning* 4.1:8–25.

Churchman, C. West. 1968. *The systems approach.* Delacorte, New York.

CIS (Counter Information Services). 1979. *The new technology.* Counter Information Services, London.

Cockburn, Cynthia. 1985a. Caught in the wheels: The high cost of being a female cog in the male machinery of engineering. In *The social*

shaping of technology, ed. Donald Mackenzie and Judy Wajcman. Open University Press, Milton Keynes.
――. 1985b. *Machinery of dominance: Women, men, and technical know-how*. Pluto, London.
――. 1986. The material of male power. In *Waged work: A reader*, ed. Feminist Review. Virago, London.
――. 1987. Restructuring technology, restructuring gender. Paper presented at the American Sociological Association Meeting, Chicago.
――. 1989. Sexual division of technology: The same again or different? In *Women, work, and computerization: Forming new alliances*, ed. K. Tijdens et al. Elsevier, Amsterdam.
Collingridge, D. 1980. *The social control of technology*. Frances Pinter, London.
Colwill, N. L. 1985. The secretarial crisis. *Business Quarterly* (Canada) 50.2:12–14.
Cooley, Mike. 1980. *Architect or bee? The human/technology relationship*. Hand and Brain, Slough, U.K.
Coombs, Rod, Paolo Saviotti, and Vivien Walsh. 1987. *Economic and technological change*. Macmillian Education, Houndmills, U.K.
Corea, Gena. 1985. *The hidden malpractice*. Harper & Row, New York.
――. 1988. *The mother machine: Reproductive technologies from artificial insemination to artificial wombs*. Women's Press, London.
――. 1989. How the new reproductive technologies will affect all women. In *Reconstructing Babylon: Women and technology*, ed. H. Patricia Hynes. Earthscan, London.
Cowan, Ruth Schwartz. 1979. From Virginia Dare to Virginia Slims: Women and technology in American life. *Technology and Culture* 20:51–63.
――. 1985. Gender and technological change. In *The social shaping of technology*, ed. Donald Mackenzie and Judy Wajcman. Open University Press, Milton Keynes.
Cramer, J., Ron Eyerman, and Andrew Jamison. 1987. The knowledge interests of the environmental movement and its potential for influencing the development of science. In *The social direction of the public sciences: Sociology of science yearbook*, ed. Stuart Blume, 9:89–115.
Crompton, R. and S. Reid. 1982. The deskilling of clerical work. In *The degradation of work? Skill, deskilling, and the labor process*, ed. S. Wood. Hutchinson, London.
Cronberg, Tarja. 1986. *Teorier om teknologi og hverdagsliv*. Nyt fra Samfundsvidenskaberne, Copenhagen.
――. 1987. Sammenfatning. In *Teknologi-opfattelser og teknologi begreber*, ed. Anne Lykkenskov. Publication 6. Teknik-Samfund Initiativet SSF, Copenhagen.
Crozier, Michel. 1971. *The world of the office worker*. University of Chicago Press, Chicago.
CSS (Council for Science and Society). 1977. *The acceptablility of risks*. Barry Rose, London.
――. 1982. *Expensive medical techniques*. Calvert's, London.
Dalton, A. 1979. *Asbestos killer dust*. BSSRS Publications, London.
Danielsen, Oluf. 1990. Teknologivurdering i Danmark: Forskning og

praksisfelt. In *Metoder i teknologivurdering erfaring og fornyelse*, ed. Tarja Cronberg and Dorte Friis. Blytmann, Copenhagen.

David, Henry P., and Janine M. Morgall. 1990. Family planning for the mentally disordered and retarded. *Journal of Nervous and Mental Disease* 178.6:385–91.

David, Henry P., Janine M. Morgall, and Niels K. Rasmussen. 1988. Family planning services delivery: Danish experience. Report of a research project prepared for the Office of Population Affairs, Washington, D.C.

David, Henry P., Janine M. Morgall, Mogens Osler, and Niels K. Rasmussen. 1990. United States and Denmark: Different approaches to health care and family planning. *Studies in Family Planning* 21.1:1–9.

Davies, M. 1974. Women's place is at the typewriter. *Radical America* 8: 1–28.

Davin, D. 1984. Expanding the secretary's role. *Managers Magazine* 59.8:40–41.

Delgado, A. 1979. *The enormous file: A social history of the office*. John Murray, London.

Dickson, David. 1984. *The new politics of science*. University of Chicago Press, Chicago.

Dinkel, Rolf H. 1985. Cost benefit analysis: A helpful tool for decision makers. *Health Policy* 4:321–30.

Dinnerstein, Dorothy. 1976. *The mermaid and the minotaur*. Harper & Row, New York.

Direcks, A. 1986. Has the DES lesson been learned? Paper given at FINRRAGE Conference, European Parliament, Brussels.

Dolkhart, Jane, and Hartstock, Nancy. 1975. Feminist visions of the future. *Quest* 2.1:2–6.

D'Onofrio-Flores, Pamela, and Sheila M. Pfafflin, eds. 1982. *Scientific-technological change and the role of women in development*. United Nations Institute for Training and Research. Westview, Boulder, Colo.

Downing, H. 1980. Word processors and the operation of women. In *The microelectronics revolution*, ed. T. Forester. Blackwell, Oxford.

Doyal, Lesley, Ken Green, Alan Irwin, Doogies Russell, Fred Steward, Robin Williams, and Dave Gee. 1983. *Cancer in Britain: The politics of prevention*. Pluto, London.

Doyal, Lesley, I. Kickbusch, and Janine M. Morgall. 1984. Women, health and development: A position paper. Unit technical paper prepared for the World Health Organization, Regional Office for Europe, March.

Duff, T. B., and P. A. Merrier. 1984. Secretaries—caught in the past? *Management World* 13.9:8–11.

Dutch Ministry of Education and Science. 1987. *Technology assessment: An opportunity for Europe*. 6 vols. European Congress on Technology Assessment, Amsterdam.

Easlea, Brian. 1980. *Witch hunting, magic, and the new philosophy: An introduction to debates of the scientific revolution, 1450–1750*. Harvester, Sussex, U.K.

———. 1981. *Science and sexual oppression: Patriarchy's confrontation with women and nature*. Weidenfeld & Nicolson, London.

———. 1983. *Fathering the unthinkable: Masculinity, scientists, and the nuclear arms race.* Pluto, London.

Edwards, Richard. 1979. *Contested terrain: The transformation of the workplace in the twentieth century.* Basic Books, New York.

Ehrenreich, Barbara, and Deirdre English. 1973. *Complaints and disorders: The sexual politics of sickness.* Glass Mountain Pamphlet 2. Feminist Press, Old Westbury, N.Y.

———. 1979. *For her own good.* Anchor Books, Garden City, N.Y.

Elling, Monica. 1984. *Paa tröskein till ett nytt liv? En reserapport fraan Storbritannien och Västtyskland.* Arbetslivscentrum, Stockholm.

Elliott, David, and Ruth Elliott. 1976. *The control of technology.* Wykeham, London.

Ellul, Jacques. 1964. *The technological society.* Vintage, New York.

Elverdam, Beth. 1984. Barnet som ikke bliver: Abort og praevention i tvaerkulturelt perspektiv. *Forum for Kvindeforskning Boernebegrænsing og Foedselskontrol* 4.1:45–52.

EMT. 1982. Expensive medical technology. London.

Esseveld, Joke. 1982. Kvinnoforskning i sökundet efter en metod. In *Teorier och metoder i kvinnoforskning,* ed. U. Broman. University of Gothenburg, Gothenburg.

Eyerman, Ron. 1985. Rationalizing intellectuals: Sweden in the 1930's and 1940's. *Theory and Society* 14:777–807.

Eyerman, Ron, and Andrew Jamison. 1991. *Social movements: A cognitive approach.* Polity Press, Cambridge.

Fahurich, K. P., A. Fauser, and N. Heller. 1984. *Extent of introduction of electronics machinery in the office.* European Foundation for the Improvement of Living and Working Conditions.

Faulkner, Wendy, and Erik Arnold, eds. 1985. *Smothered by invention: Technology in women's lives.* Pluto, London.

Feibleman, James K. 1972. Pure science, applied science, technology, engineering: An attempt at definitions. In *Technology and society,* ed. Noel de Nevers. Addison-Wesley, Reading, Mass.

Feldberg, Roslyn, and Evelyn Glenn. 1983. Technology and work degradation. In *Machina ex dea: Feminist perspectives on technology,* ed. Joan Rothschild. Pergamon, Elmsford, N.Y.

———. 1987. Technology and the transformation of clerical work. In *Technology and the transformation of white collar work,* ed. Robert Kraut. Lawrence Erlbaun, Hillsdale, N.J.

Feldman, Rayah. 1987. The politics of the new reproduction technologies. *Critical Social Policy* 7.1.

Feminist Review, ed. 1986. *Waged work: A reader.* Virago, London.

Firestone, Shulamith. 1970. *The dialectics of sex.* Bantam, New York.

Fischer, Frank. 1990. *Technocracy and the politics of expertise.* Sage, Newbury Park, Calif.

Folketingets Finansudvalg. 1982. *Aktstykke* 129.14.

Foucault, Michel. 1973. *The birth of the clinic: An archaeology of medical perception.* Tavistock, London.

———. 1980. *The history of sexuality,* vol. 1, *An introduction.* Vintage, New York.

Fox Keller, Evelyn. 1985. *Reflections on gender and science.* Yale University Press, New Haven, Conn.

Frankel, C. 1973. The nature and sources of irrationalism. *Science,* 1 June, pp. 927–31.

233   Bibliography

Frankfort, Ellen. 1973. *Vaginal politics*. Bantam, New York.
Freidson, Eliot. 1970. *The profession of medicine: A study in the sociology of applied knowledge*. Dodd Mead, New York.
———. 1980. *Doctoring together: A study of professional social control*. University of Chicago Press, Chicago.
Fremskridtets Pris. 1984. Indenrigsministeret, Copenhagen.
Freund, J. 1966. *The sociology of Max Weber*. Penguin, London.
Fuchs, V. 1968. The growing demand for medical care. *New England Journal of Medicine* 279.4:190–95.
Gartner, Alan. 1982. The consumer in the service society. In *Developing consumer health information services*, ed. Alan M. Rees. Bowker, New York.
Gearhart, Sally. 1983. An end to technology: A modest proposal. In *Machina ex dea: Feminist perspectives on technology*, ed. Joan Rothschild. Pergamon, Elmsford, N.Y.
Gibbons, John H., and Holly L. L. Gwin. 1988. Techology and governance: The development of the Office of Technology Assessment. In *Technology and politics*, ed. Michael E. Kraft and Normon J. Vig. Duke University Press, Durham, N.C.
Giddens, Anthony. 1989. *Sociology*. Polity, Oxford.
Gilligan, Carol. 1982. *In a different voice: Psychological theory and women's development*. Harvard University Press, Cambridge, Mass.
Giuliano, Vincent. 1982. The mechanization of office work. *Scientific America*, September 1982, pp. 125–34.
Goldhaber, Michael. 1980. Politics and technology: Micro-processors and the prospect of a new industrial revolution. *Socialist Review* 10.53:9–32.
Goransson, Anita. 1978. Den konsliga arbetsdelninge och dens strategiska konsekvenser. *Sociologisk Froskning* 15.3:51–81.
Gordon, Linda. 1974. *Women's body, women's right*. Penguin, Harmondsworth.
———. 1977. *Women's body, women's right: A social history of birth control in America*. Penguin, New York.
Gray, Elizabeth Dodson. 1979. *Why the green nigger? Remything Genesis*. Roundtable, Wellesley, Mass.
Greenbaum, Joan. 1976. Division of labor in the computer field. In *Technology: The labor process and the working class*. Monthly Review Press, New York.
Greve, Rose Marie. 1987. Women and information technology: A European overview. In *Women and information technology*, ed. M. J. Davidson and C. L. Cooper. Wiley, New York.
Griffin, Susan. 1978. *Women and nature: The roaring inside her*. Harper & Row, New York.
Habermas, Jürgen. 1972. *Knowledge and human interests*. Heinemann, London.
Hacker, Sally. 1989. *Pleasure, power, and technology*. Unwin Hyman, Boston.
Hagerty, Eileen M., and Joan E. Tighe. 1978. Office automation and the clerical worker. Paper presented at MIT lecture series Technology and work: The worker's perspective, Cambridge, Mass.
Hansen, Ebba Holme, and Laila Launsoe. 1987. Clinical trials: Towards a different model. *Journal of Clinical Pharmacy* 6:67–74.
———. 1989. Is the controlled clinical trial sufficient as a drug technol-

ogy assessment? *Journal of Social and Administrative Pharmacy* 6.3: 117–26.
Hansen, Ebba Holme, Laila Launsoe, and Janine M. Morgall. 1989. *Forsoeg, Laering, evaluering: Samarbejde mellem brugerorganisationer & apoteksfarmaceuter om laegemiddelanvendelse.* Institut for Samfundsfarmaci, Copenhagen.
Hardin, Garrett. 1972. The tragedy of the commons. In *Technology and Society*, ed. Noel de Nevers. Addison-Wesley, Reading, Mass.
Harman, Chris. 1974. *Is a machine after your job?* SWP, London.
Harris, Louis, and Associates. 1978. *Health maintenance: A nationwide survey of the barriers to better health and ways of overcoming them: Conducted among representative samples of the American public, business, and labor.* Pacific Mutual Life Insurance Co., Newport Beach, Calif.
Hartmann, Heidi. 1979. Capitalism, patriarchy, and job segregation by sex. In *Capitalist patriarchy and the case for socialist feminism*, ed. Zillah Eisenstein. Monthly Review Press, New York.
———. 1981. The unhappy marriage of Marxism and feminism: Towards a more progressive union. In *Women and revolution*, ed. Lydia Sargent. South End Press, Boston.
Hartsock, Nancy. 1983. The feminist standpoint: Developing the ground for a specifically feminist historical materialism. In *Discovering reality: Feminist perspectives on epistemology, metaphysics, methodology, and philosophy of science*, ed. Sandra Harding and Merrill Hintikka. Reidel, Dordrecht.
Henderson, Hazel. 1975. Philosophical conflict: Re-examining the goals of knowledge. *Public Administration Review*, January–February, pp. 77–80.
Hensen, C. T. 1980. Word processing opens doors for women. *Management World* 9.6:29–30.
Herborg, Hanne. 1989. Interview. Royal Danish School of Pharmacy, Institute for Social Pharmacy, Copenhagen.
Hetman, François. 1973. *Society and the assessment of technology.* OECD, Paris.
Hilden, K., A. Houe, J. Morgall, and I. Stauning. 1981. Kvinder, utopi, teknologi. *Naturkampen*, no. 21:20–23.
Hoffmeyer, Jesper. 1982. *Samfundets Naturhistorie.* Rosinante, Copenhagen.
Hoos, Ida. 1982. *A critical assessment of existing technology practices.* IFA Information Day. Handelshoejskolen, Copenhagen.
Huws, Ursula. 1982. *Your job in the eighties: A women's guide to new technology.* Pluto, London.
Hynes, Patricia. 1987. A paradigm for regulation of the biomedical industry in the U.S. In *Made to order: The myth of reproductive and genetic progress*, ed. Patricia Spallone and Debora Steinberg. Pergamon, Oxford.
———, ed. 1989a. *Reconstructing Babylon: Women and technology.* Earthscan, London.
———. 1989b. *The recurring silent spring.* Pergamon, London.
IJTAHC. 1989. Technology assessment reports. *International Journal of Technology Assessment in Health Care* 5:137–53.
ILO (International Labor Office). 1985a. *Equal opportunities and*

equal treatment for men and women in employment. Report 7, International Labor Conference, 71st sess. ILO, Geneva.

————. 1985b. *Technological change: The tripartite response.* ILO Geneva.

IMI (Irish Managers Institute). *Microcomputers in the administration of management processes in smaller businesses.* IMI, Dublin.

Institute of Medicine. 1985. *Assessing medical technology.* National Academy Press, Washington, D.C.

Ipsen, S. 1985. Tidsstrukturer og flexibilitet i kvinders hverdagsliv. In *Teknologi og kvinders hverdag.* Institut for Erhversv-og Samfundsforskning, Handelshøjskolen, Copenhagen.

Irwin, A. 1985. *Risk and control of technology.* Manchester University Press, Manchester, U.K.

Iversen, Lars. 1990. *Virksomhedslukninger, arbejdsløshed og helbred.* Publication 23. Institut for Socialmedicin og FADLs Forlag, Copenhagen.

Jamison, Andrew. 1990. *Science and technology policy: Theory and history.* Course lectures, January–February. Research Policy Institute, Lund.

Jamison, Andrew, and Erik Baark. 1990. Modes of biotechnology assessment in the USA, Japan, and Denmark. *Technology Analysis and Strategic Management* 2.2:111–27.

Jantsch, Eric. 1967. *Technological forecasting in perspective.* OECD, Paris.

Joergensen, Eva. 1986. Teknologivurdering—dens sigte og grundlag. In *Metoder i teknologivurdering,* ed. Tarja Cronberg. Publication 5, Teknik-Samfund Initiativet. Statens Samfundsvidenskablig Forskningsraad, Copenhagen.

Kanter, Rosabeth Moss. 1977. *Men and women of the corporation.* Basic Books, New York.

Kasper, Anne S. 1985. Hysterectomy as social progress. *Women and Health* 10.1:109–27.

Kendall, B. 1979. Ascension of the supersecretary. *Canadian Business* 51:116–20.

Kinnersly, Patrick. 1974. *The hazards of work: How to fight them.* Pluto, London.

Kirejczyk, Marta. 1988. Does feminist technology assessment make sense? Paper presented at 4 S EASST Conference, Amsterdam, 17 November.

————. 1990. A question of meaning? Controversies about the new reproductive technologies in the Netherlands. *Issues in Reproductive and Genetic Engineering* 3.1:22–33.

Kittay, Eva Feder. 1984. Womb envy: An explanatory concept. In *Mothering: Essays in feminist theory,* ed. Joyce Trebilcot. Rowman & Allenheld, Totowa, N.J.

Klein, Renate, ed. 1989. *Infertility: Women speak out about their experiences of reproductive medicine.* Pandora, London.

Koch, Lene. 1986. Kvinder og forplantnings teknologi. *Forum for Kvindeforskning* 6.4:49–52.

————. 1989. *Oenskeboern: Kvinder og reagensglasbefrugtning.* Rosinante, Copenhagen.

Koch, Lene, and Janine M. Morgall. 1987. Towards a feminist assessment of reproductive technology. *Acta Sociologica* 2:173–91.

Kolmos, Anette. 1989. Koennet i ingenioerviden. In *Koen og Videnskab*. Aalborg University Press, Aalborg.

Korvajärvi, Päivi. 1989. New technology and gendered division of labor. In *Women, work, and computerization: Forming new alliances*, ed. K. Tijdens et al. Elsevier, Amsterdam.

Kraft, P. 1979. The industrialization of computer programming: From programming to software production. In *Case studies on the labor process*, ed. A. Zimbalist. Monthly Review Press, New York.

Kraft, P., and S. Dubnoff. 1984. Software for women means a lower status. In *Smothered by invention: Technology in women's lives*, ed. Wendy Faulkner and Erik Arnold. Pluto, London.

Kramarae, Cheris, ed. 1988. *Technology and women's voices: Keeping in touch*. Routledge & Kegan Paul, New York.

Kuhn, Thomas. 1970. *The structure of scientific revolution*. University of Chicago Press, Chicago.

Kvande, Elin. 1982. Anpassning och protest. *Kvinnovetenskaplig Tidskrift*, no. 3:42–51.

Launsoe, Laila. 1991. The demands for qualitative research are developing. *Journal of Social and Administrative Pharmacy* 8.1:1–6.

Launsoe, Laila, and Olaf Rieper. 1987. *Forskning om og med Mennesker*. Nyt Nordisk Forlag Arnold Busch, Copenhagen.

Lauritzen, Wenche. 1990. *Naturvidenskabens og teknikkens maskuline dominans*. Forlaget Sociologi, Copenhagen.

Lehto, Anna-Maija. 1989. Women's labor market position from the perspective of technological change. In *Women, work, and computerization: Forming new alliances*, ed. K. Tijdens et al. Elsevier, Amsterdam.

Leira, H. 1987. Temanummer om barnløshed. *Nytt om Kvinneforskning*. NAVF, Oslo.

Ligestillingsraadet. 1987. *Aarsberetning 1986*. Ligestillingsraadet, Copenhagen.

Liljestroem, R. 1979. *Kultur och arbete*. Sekretariatet för Fremtidsstudier, Stockholm.

Lloyd, Anne, and Liz Newell. 1985. Women and computers. In *Smothered by invention: Technology in women's lives*, ed. Wendy Faulkner and Erik Arnold. Pluto, London.

Lockwood, David. 1958. *The blackcoated worker*. Allen & Unwin, London.

Lund, Anker Brink, and Jytte Moeller Christensen. 1986. *Kommunikation i sundhedsvaesenet: Problemer, behov og visioner*. Public Information Paper 7/86. Kommunikationsuddannelsen, Roskilde University Center, Roskilde.

MacKenzie, Donald, and Judy Wajcman, eds. 1987. *The social shaping of technology*. Open University Press, Milton Keynes.

McKinlay, John B. 1981. From "promising report" to "standard procedure": Seven stages in the career of a medical innovation. *Milbank Memorial Fund: Quality, Health, and Society* 59.3:274–411.

Madison, Mary Ann, and Varyt Coates. 1989. Women, work and technology: The labor market. In *Women, work and computerization: Forming new alliances*, ed. K. Tijdens et al. Elsevier, Amsterdam.

Major, M. J. 1984. Partners . . . or pawns? *Modern Office Technology*, June, pp. 96–104.

Manpower Ltd. 1985. *Users' experience in office automation*. Manpower Temporary Services, Slough, U.K.

Marcuse, Herbert. 1964. *One-dimensional man.* Beacon, Boston.
Markoff, John, and Jon Stewart. 1979. The microprocessor revolution: An office on the head of a pin. *These Times*, March, pp. 7–13.
Meadows, Donella H., Dennis L. Meadows, Joergen Randers, and William Behrens. 1974. *The limits to growth: A report for the Club of Rome's Project on the Predicament of Mankind.* Pan Books, London.
Merchant, Carolyn. 1980. *The death of nature: Women, ecology, and the scientific revolution.* Harper & Row, New York.
———. 1981. Out of the past: Women and nature. *Future, Technology, and Women*, March, pp. 6–8.
Messing, Karen. 1983. The scientific mystique: Can a white lab coat guarantee purity in the search for knowledge about the nature of women? In *Women's nature: Rationalizations of inequality*, ed. Marian Lowe and Ruth Hubbard. Pergamon, New York.
Meyer, Gitte. 1991. Oekonomisk stimulans eller etisk barrier. *Teknologi Debat* 1:191.
Mills, C. Wright. 1951. *White collar.* Oxford University Press, London.
———. 1959. *The sociological imagination.* Oxford University Press, New York.
Mitchell, G. Duncan. 1968. *A dictionary of sociology.* Routledge & Kegan Paul, London.
Moeller, Kim. 1986. Fra roed til groen: Om tanker der blev vaek. In *Metoder i teknologivurdering*, ed. Tarja Cronberg. Publikation 5, Teknik-Samfund Initiativet. Statens Samfundsvidenskablig Forskningsraad, Copenhagen.
Mooney, Gavin H., Elizabeth M. Russell, and Roy D. Weir. 1980. *Choices for health care: Studies in social policy.* Macmillan, London.
Morgall, Janine M. 1980. Epoxy boycott in Denmark: Fight for a safe workplace. *Science for the People*, September–October, pp. 22–26.
———. 1981a. Hvor er kvinderne henne i teknologi debatten? *Kvinder*, no. 40 (October–November): 4–6. (In Danish.)
———. 1981b. Kontrol med anslagene: Anslag mod kontrollen. *Naturkampen*, no. 20: 16–19. (In Danish.)
———. 1981c. Med tangentvalsen mot friheten eller kan den nya kontortekniken frigora kvinnora? *Kvinnovetenskaplig Tidskrift*, no. 1–2:31–42. (In Swedish.)
———. 1982a. How work organization affects health: Women and new technology in the office. Paper presented at Workshop on Employment Patterns in the Eighties, Helsinki, July.
———. 1982b. Hvorfor bliver vi syge? *Kvinder*, no. 44 (June–July): 28–29. (In Danish.)
———. 1982c. Kvinder siger ikke noget . . . de finder sig bare i det . . . vel gaar vi ej!! *Kvinder*, no. 47 (December): 18–19. (In Danish.)
———. 1982d. Oplaeg til folketingshoring om "*Fagre nye telehverdag.*" Background paper for Danish Parliamentary Hearing on New Technology, March. (In Danish.)
———. 1982e. Review of M. Craig, *Office workers' survival handbook.* In *Economic and Industrial Democracy* 3.4:124–28.
———. 1982f. Typing our way to freedom: New office technology. *The changing experience of women*, ed. Elizabeth Whitelegg et al. Martin Robertson, Oxford.

————. 1983a. Findes den teknologiske kvinde? *Forum for Kvindeforskning* 3.2:5–14. (In Danish.)

————. 1983b. Kontorautomatisering set ud fra et kvindeperspektiv. In *Informationsteknologien og Kommunestyret.* Den Kommunale Hoejskole, Copenhagen. (In Danish.)

————. 1983c. Strengthening group solidarity of clericals: A case study in office automation. In *Office automation,* ed. Daniel Marshall and Judith Gregory. Working Women Education Fund, Cleveland.

————. 1984a. Le donne e la salute e piu della salute delle donne. *La Salute Umana* 71.5:5–9. (In Italian.)

————. 1984b. Health for all by the year 2000: The role of health education. In *Health promotion is no easy job: Introducing the Health Education Unit.* World Health Organization, Regional Office for Europe, Copenhagen.

————. 1984c. Meeting report: International workshop on women and health documentation centres in Europe. *Health Libraries Review* 1.3:170–71.

————. 1984d. Women and health in Europe. *World Health: The magazine of the World Health Organization.* April. (In English, Spanish, and French.)

————. 1985. Women and depression. *Euro News,* no. 10:4–9.

————. 1986. New office technology. In *Waged work: A reader,* ed. Feminist Review. Virago, London.

————. 1987. Family planning services and the mentally ill: An interview with psychiatric personnel. In *Sexuality and family planning: Perspectives for the mentally ill and handicapped.* Publication 6. Danish Family Planning Association, Copenhagen.

————. 1988a. *Evaluering: Tvaerfagligt samarbejde—Forbedret seksualundervisning.* Kalundborg, Report prepared for Kalundborg Kommune. (In Danish.)

————. 1988b. "Medical experiments: Women's bodies as living laboratories?" Paper prepared for the seminar "Experimenting Health," Turin, Italy, November.

Morgall, Janine M., Ebba Holme Hansen, and Laila Launsoe. 1988. Integrating the user's perspective into technology assessment. Paper prepared for the fourth annual meeting of the International Society of Technology Assessment in Health Care, Boston.

Morgall, Janine M., and Niels K. Rasmussen. 1987. *Family planning service delivery: State of the art, Denmark, 1986.* Institute for Social Medicine, University of Copenhagen, Copenhagen.

Morgall, Janine M., and Gitte Vedel. 1985. Office Automation. *Economic and Industrial Democracy* 6.1:93–112.

Müller, Jens, Arne Remmen, and Per Christensen. 1986. *Samfundets teknologi teknologiens samfund.* Systime, Herning.

Mumford, E. 1983. *Designing secretaries.* Manchester Business School, Manchester, U.K.

Mumford, Lewis. 1966, 1970. *The myth of the machine,* vol. 1, *Technics and human development*; vol. 2, *The pentagon of power.* Harcourt Brace Jovanovich, New York.

Murphy, John W. 1987. A Weberian approach to technology assessment. *Quarterly Journal of Ideology* 11.2:67–74.

Murphy, Julien S. 1989. Should pregnancies be sustained in brain-dead women? A philosophical discussion of postmortem pregnancy. In

Healing technology: Feminist perspectives, ed. Kathryn Strother Ratcliff. University of Michigan Press, Ann Arbor.

Nandy, Ashis. 1979. The traditions of technology. *Alternatives* 4.3:371–86.

Navarro, V. 1977. *Medicine under capitalism*. Croom Helm, London.

NEDO (National Economic Development Office). 1983. *The impact of advanced information systems: The effect on job content and job boundaries*. NEDO, London.

Nelkin, Dorothy. 1977. *The politics of participation*. Sage, Beverly Hills, Calif.

———, ed. 1979. Science, technology, and political conflict: Analyzing the issues. In *Controversy: Politics of technological decisions*. Sage, London.

Newman, Elkie. 1985. Who controls birth control? In *Smothered by Invention: Technology in women's lives*, ed. Wendy Faulkner and Erik Arnold. Pluto, London.

Noble, David. 1977. *America by design: Science, technology, and the rise of corporate capitalism*. Knopf, New York.

———. 1979. Social choice in machine design: The case of automatically controlled machine tools. In *Case studies on the labor process*, ed. Andrew Zimbalist. Monthly Review Press, New York.

———. 1986. *Forces of production: A social history of industrial automation*. Oxford University Press, New York.

———. 1992a. A world without women. *Technology Review*, May–June, pp. 54–60.

———. 1992b. *A world without women: The clerical culture of western science*. Knopf, New York.

Nyemark, Niels. 1989. *Laegemiddelpriser og oekonomisk farmakoterapi*. Forskningsrapport 4. Odense Universitet Institut for Sundhedsoekonomi og Sygdomsforebyggelse, Odense.

Oakley, Ann. 1980. *Women confined: Toward a sociology of childbirth*. Schocken, New York.

———. 1987. From walking wombs to test-tube babies. In *Reproductive technologies: Gender, motherhood, and medicine*, ed. Michelle Stanworth. Polity, Cambridge.

———. 1990. Who's afraid of the randomized controlled trial? Some dilemmas of the scientific method and "good" research practices. In *Doing feminist research*, ed. Helen Roberts. Routledge & Kegan Paul, London.

Oakley, Ann, and Susanne Houd. 1990. *Helpers in childbirth: Midwifery today*. Hemisphere, New York.

OECD (Organization for Economic Cooperation and Development). 1971. *Science, growth and society*. OECD, Paris.

———. 1973. *Society and the assessment of technology*. OECD, Paris.

———. 1975. *Methodological guidelines for social assessment of technology*. OECD, Paris.

———. 1978. *Social assessment of technology*. OECD, Paris.

———. 1979. *Technology on trial: Public participation in decision-making related to science and technology*. OECD, Paris.

———. 1981. *Information activities: Electronics and telecommunication technologies*. OECD, Paris.

———. 1983. *Assessing the impact of technology on society*. OECD, Paris.

————. 1985. *Measuring health care, 1960–1983: Expenditure costs and performance.* OECD, Paris.

Ogburn, W. F. 1950. *On culture and social change.* University of Chicago Press, Chicago.

Olsten, W. 1982. Secretaries and the new technology. *Supervisory Management* 27.10:31–35.

Osler, Mogens, Janine M. Morgall, and Birgitte Jensen. 1990. *Repeat abortion: The Danish experience.* Sexuality and Family Planning Unit, World Health Organization, Copenhagen.

————. 1992. Repeat abortion in Denmark. *Danish Medical Bulletin* 39:89–91.

Osler, Mogens, Henry P. David, Janine M. Morgall, and Niels K. Rasmussen. 1990. Family planning services delivery: Danish experience. *Danish Medical Bulletin* 37:95–105.

OTA (Office of Technology Assessment). 1972. *Hearing before the subcommittee on computer services.* U.S. Senate Committee on Rules and Administration, Washington, D.C.

————. 1980. *The implications of cost-effectiveness analysis of medical technology.* U.S. Government Printing Office, Washington, D.C.

Otway, H. J., and Peltu, M., eds. 1983. *New office technology: Human and organisational aspects.* Frances Pinter, London.

Pacey, Arnold. 1983. *The culture of technology.* Basil Blackwell, Oxford.

Patton, Michael Quinn. 1990. *Qualitative evaluation and research methods.* Sage, Newbury Park, Calif.

Perry, S. 1987. Technology assessment in health care in the United States. Paper presented at the TEKMED 87 Conference on Health for All in the Future, Lyon, May.

Petersen, Birgit. 1984. Praevention er politik: Ogsaa koenspolitik. *Forum for Kvindeforskning* 4.1:53–63.

Piercy, Marge. 1976. *Woman on the edge of time.* Fawcett Crest, New York.

Polak, Fred P. 1971. *Prognostics.* Amsterdam.

Rasmussen, Niels K. 1983. *Abort—et valg? Fødsler, fødslsbegraensning og svangerskabsafbrydelse: Baggrund og aarsager til udviklingen i aborttallet.* FADL's forlag (Publication of the Institute for Social Medicine). University of Copenhagen, Copenhagen.

Rasmussen, Niels K., and Janine M. Morgall. 1990. The use of alternative treatments in the Danish adult population. *Complementary Medical Research,* June, pp. 16–22.

Ratcliff, Kathryn Strother, ed. 1989. *Healing technology: Feminist perspectives.* University of Michigan Press, Ann Arbor.

Raymond, Janice G. 1989. Of eggs, embryos, and altruism. In *Reconstructing Babylon: Women and technology,* ed. Patricia Hynes. Earthscan, London.

Rees, Alan M., ed. 1982. *Developing consumer health information services.* Bowker, New York.

Reeves, Richard. 1988. Video war: Garbage in, garbage out, and cross your fingers. *International Herald Tribune,* July 7.

Reisner, Stanley Joel. 1978. *Medicine and the reign of technology.* Cambridge University Press, London.

Reissman, Catherine Kohler. 1983. Women and medicalization: A new perspective. *Social Policy* 14.1 (3–18).

Remmen, Arne. 1986. Teknologivurdering: Eller historien om "kej-

serens nye klaeder." In *Metoder i teknologivurdering*, ed. Tarja Cronberg. Publication 5, Teknik-Samfund Initiativet. Statens Samfundsvidenskablig Forskningsraad, Copenhagen.
————. 1991. At komme bagklogskaben i forkøbet. *Teknologi Debat*, no. 2:22–24.
Rich, A. 1977. *Of women born: Motherhood as experience and institution.* Virago, London.
Roberts, Helen. 1981. Women and their doctors: Power and powerlessness in the research process. In *Doing feminist research*, ed. Helen Roberts. Routledge & Kegan Paul, London.
Rose, Hilary. 1982. Making science feminist. In *The changing experience of women*, ed. Elizabeth Whitelegg et al. Martin Robertson, Oxford.
————. 1983. Hand, brain, and heart: Towards a feminist epistemology for the sciences. *Signs* 9:73–90.
————. 1986. Beyond masculinist realities: A feminist epistemology for the sciences. In *Feminist approaches to science*, ed. Ruth Bleier. Pergamon, Elmsford, N.Y.
————. 1987. Victorian values, in the test-tube: The politics of reproductive science and technology. In *Reproductive technologies: Gender, motherhood, and medicine*, ed. Michelle Stanworth. Polity, Cambridge.
Rose, Hilary, and S. Rose, eds. 1976. *Ideology of/in the natural sciences.* Schenkman, Boston.
Rossiter, Margaret W. 1979. Women scientists in America before 1920. In *Dynamos and virgins revisited: Women and technological change in history*, ed. Martha Moore Trescott. Scarecrow, Metuchen, N.J.
Roszak, Theodore. 1974. The monster and the titan: Science, knowledge, and gnosis. *Daedalus*, Summer, p. 1732.
Rothschild, Joan. 1981. Review of *The death of nature. Women's Studies International Quarterly* 4.3:305–12.
————, ed. 1983. *Machina ex dea: Feminist perspectives on technology.* Pergamon, Elmsford, N.Y.
Royal Society of Arts Examination Board. 1981. *Office technology: The implications for education and training in the 1980's*. RSA, London.
Russ, Joanna. 1975. *The female man.* Bantam Books, New York.
Rybczynski, Witold. 1983. *Taming the tiger: The struggle to control technology.* Viking, New York.
Salomon, Jean-Jacques. 1988. Technology and democracy. In *From research policy to social intelligence*, ed. Jan Annerstedt and Andrew Jamison. Macmillan, London.
Schot, Johan. 1992. Constructive technology assessment and technology dynamics: Opportunities for the control of technology—the case of clean technology. *Science, Technology, and Human Values* 17:36–56.
Seal, Vivien. 1990. *Whose choice? Working class women and the control of fertility.* Fortress Books, London.
Sidenius, Katrine. 1986. Et matriarkat uden maend. *Forum for Kvindeforskning* 6.4:54–55.
Silverston, R. 1976. Office work for women: An historical perspective. *Business History* 18:98–110.
Silverston, R., and R. Towler, 1984. Secretaries at work. *Ergonomics* 27.5:557–64.

Smith, Judy. 1981. Into the future: Women and nature. In *Future, technology, and women*. San Diego State University, San Diego, Calif.
Smits, Ruud, and Jos Leyten. 1988. Key issues in the institutions of TA: Development of TA in five European countries and USA. *Futures*, February, pp. 19–36.
Softley, Elena. 1985. Word processing: New opportunities for women office workers. In *Smothered by invention: Technology in women's lives*, ed. Wendy Faulkner and Erik Arnold. Pluto, London.
Solomon, Alison. 1989. Infertility as crisis: Coping, surviving and thriving. In *Infertility: Women speak out about their experiences of reproductive medicine*, ed. Renate D. Klein. Pandora, London.
Spallone, Patricia, and Debora Steinberg, eds. 1987. *Made to order: The myth of reproductive and genetic progress*. Pergamon, Oxford.
SPRU (Science Policy Research Unit). 1982. Microelectronics and women's employment. In *Britain, women, and technology studies*. SPRU Occasional Paper Series 17. University of Sussex, Sussex.
Standke, Klaus-Heinrich. 1986. Technology assessment: An essentially political process. *Impact of Science on Society*, no. 141:65–76.
Stanley, Autumn. 1981. Daughters of Isis, daughters of Demeter: When women sowed and reaped. *Women's Studies International Quarterly* 4.3:289–304.
Stanworth, Michelle, ed. 1987. *Reproductive technologies: Gender, motherhood, and medicine*. Polity, Cambridge.
Starr, Chauncey. 1972. Social benefit versus technological risk. In *Technology and society*, ed. Noel de Nevers. Addison-Wesley, Reading, Mass.
Starr, Paul. 1982. *The social transformation of American medicine*. Basic Books, New York.
Stein, D. 1985. *Ada: A life and legacy*. MIT Press, Cambridge, Mass.
STG (Stuurgroep Toekomstscenario's Gezondheidzorg). 1987. *Anticipating and assessing health care technology*, vol. 1, *General considerations and policy conclusions*. Martinus Nijhoff, Dordrecht.
Swedish National Board of Occupational Safety and Health. 1981. *Asbestos and inorganic fibres*. Criteria Document for Swedish Occupational Standards. Stockholm.
Taylor, Shelley. 1986. *Health psychology*. Random House, New York.
Teknologiraadet. 1980. *Teknologivurdering i Danmark*. Teknologiraadet, Juni.
Teknologistyrelsen. 1984. *Organisering af teknologivurdering i Danmark: Erfaringer og perspektiver*. Teknologistyrelsen, Copenhagen.
Thompson, Paul. 1983. *The nature of work: An introduction to debates on the labor process*. Macmillan Education, London.
Tisdell, C. A. 1981. *Science and technology policy: Priorities of governments*. Chapman & Hall, London.
Trescott, Martha Moor, ed. 1979. *Dynamos and virgins revisited: Women and technological change in history*. Scarecrow, Metuchen, N.J.
Tuininga, E. J. 1988. Technology assessment in Europe. *Futures*, February, pp. 37–45.
U.S. Congress, House Committee on Science and Technology. 1966. *Side-effects of technological innovation*. 89th Cong., 2d sess.
———, House Committee on Science and Astronautics. 1969. *Technology: Processes of assessment and choice*. Report of the Academy of Sciences. 91st Cong., 1st sess.

Vanderwater, Bette. 1992. Meanings and strategies of reproductive control: Current feminist approaches to reproductive technology. *Issues in Reproductive and Genetic Engineering* 5.3:215–30.

Veatch, R. M. 1981. The medical model: Its nature and problems. In *Concepts of health and disease: Interdisciplinary perspectives*, ed. A. L. Caplan, H. T. Engehardt, and J. J. McCartney. Addison, London.

Vedel, Gitte. 1982. *Om Kvindearbejdets igangvaerende udvikling og perspektiver: I relation til den teknologiske udvikling.* Institut for Geografi, Samfundsanalyse og Datalogi Arbejdspapir 25. Roskilde University Center, Roskilde.

———. 1986. *Ude af oeje, ude af sind: Om kvinders distance arbejde.* Samfundslitteratur, Gylling.

Vedel, Gitte, and Janine M. Morgall. 1983a. Kvindeperspektiver paa teknologivurdering. *Samfundsoekonomen* 1:17–23. (In Danish.)

———. 1983b. Nyteknik og kontorarbejder. In *Teknik-hverdagsliv.* Danish Research Council Committee for Technology and Society, Copenhagen. (In Danish.)

Vinnicombe, S. 1980. *Secretaries, management, and organisations.* Heinemann, London.

Wad, Atul, and Michael Radnor. 1984. *Technology assessment: Review and implications for developing countries.* UNESCO, Paris.

Wagner, Marsden. 1986. "The appropriate use of repoductive technology." Speech at the First Feminist European Conference on Reproductive Technology and Genetic Engineering, Palma de Mallorca, October.

Waitzkin, Howard. 1978. A Marxist view of medical care. *Science for the People*, November–December, pp. 31–41.

Waitzkin, Howard, and Waterman, B. 1974. *The exploitation of illness in capitalist society.* Bobbs-Merrill, Indianapolis.

Wajcman, Judy. 1991. *Feminism confronts technology.* Polity, Cambridge.

Wajcman, Judy, and B. Probert. 1988. New technology outwork. In *Technology and the labor process: Australian case studies*, ed. E. Willis. Allen & Unwin, Sydney.

Walden, Louise. 1982. Teknikkulturens dubbla fortecken. *Kvinnovetenskaplig Tidsskrift* 3.

———. 1990. Genom Symaskinens nålsäga: Teknik och social förändring i kvinnokultur och manskultur. Diss., Linköping University.

Waldron, Ingrid. 1977. Increased prescribing of Valium, Librium, and other drugs: An example of the influences of economic and social factors on the practice of medicine. *International Journal of Health Services* 7.1:37–62.

Walsh, V. 1980. Contraception: The growth of a technology. In *Alice through the microscope: The power of science over women's lives*, ed. Lynda Birke, Wendy Faulkner, and Kathy Ovenfield. Virago, London.

Warner, Deborah J. 1979. Women inventors at the centennial. In *Dynamos and virgins revisited: Women and technological change in history*, ed. Martha M. Trescott. Scarecrow, Metuchen, N.J.

Webster, Juliet. 1989. Influencing the content of women's work in automated offices. In *Women, work, and computerization: Forming new alliances*, ed. K. Tijdens et al. Elsevier, Amsterdam.

Weinberg, Alvin M. 1972. Can technology replace social engineering? In *Technology and society*, ed. Noel de Nevers. Addison-Wesley, Reading, Mass.

Werneke, D. 1983. *Microelectronics and office jobs: The impact of machines on women's employment*. ILO, Geneva.

Whitelegg, Elizabeth, Madeleine Arnot, Else Bartels, Veronica Beechey, Lynda Birke, Susan Himmelweit, Diana Leonard, Sonja Ruehl, and Mary Anne Speakman, eds. 1982. *The changing experience of women*. Martin Robertson, Oxford.

Wilkinson, Barry. 1983. *The shopfloor politics of new technology*. Heinemann, London.

Willis, Paul. 1979. *Learning to labor*. Gower, Hampshire, U.K.

Winkler, L. 1985. Role reversal in the executive suite. *International Management Europe* 40.10:82–84.

Winner, Langdon. 1977. *Autonomous technology: Technics out-of-control as a theme in political thought*. MIT Press, Cambridge, Mass.

———. 1986. *The whale and the reactor: A search for limits in an age of high technology*. University of Chicago Press, Chicago.

Wright, Barbara Drygulski, et al. 1987. *Women, work, and technology: Transformations*. University of Michigan Press, Ann Arbor.

Wynne, B. 1975. The rhetoric of consensus politics: A critical review of technology assessment. *Research Policy* 4:108–58.

Yanoshik, Kim, and Judy Norsigian. 1989. Contraception, control, and choice: International perspectives. In *Healing technologies: Feminist perspectives*, ed. Kathryn Strother Ratcliff. University of Michigan Press, Ann Arbor.

Young, Iris. 1981. Beyond the unhappy marriage: A critique of the dual systems theory. In *Women and revolution*, ed. Lydia Sargent. South End Press, Boston.

Zimmerman, Jan, ed. 1983. *The technological woman: Interfacing with tomorrow*. Praeger, New York.

———. 1986. *Once upon the future: A woman's guide to tomorrow's technology*. Pandora, New York.

Zimmerman, Mary K. 1987. The women's health movement: A critique of medical enterprise and the position of women. In *Analyzing gender: A handbook of social sciences research*, ed. Beth B. Hess and Myra Marx Ferree. Sage, Beverly Hills, Calif.

Zmroczek, Chris, and Felicity Henwood. 1983. *New information technology and women's employment*. FAST Occasional Paper 54. European Community, Brussels.

Index